This Basic Bible Series study was developed through the combined efforts and resources of a number of David C. Cook's dedicated lesson writers. It was compiled and edited by Frederick Bazzoli, designed by Melanie Lawson and Dawn Lauck, with cover art by Richard Sparks. —Gary Wilde, Series Editor

Scripture taken from the HOLY BIBLE, NEW INTERNATIONAL VERSION. © 1973, 1978, 1984 International Bible Society. Used by permission of Zondervan Bible Publishers.

ISBN: 1-55513-851-9
Library of Congress Catalog Number: 87-70314

I Corinthians 1:2

To those sanctified in Christ Jesus
and called to be holy.

Contents

Contents

The Christian in Community

Christian "community" today comes in many shapes and sizes. Some Christians live together in the same house, sharing cars, household chores, joys, and sorrows. Others live in separate homes but have worked out plans for sharing resources, so that every home does not need to have such items as ladders or washing machines.

Some Christians meet only for spiritual sharing around the Bible, either in small groups or large ones. Others seek to bare their souls in a "growth group" or "task force" they believe will support them in their efforts to serve Christ.

Whatever form Christian fellowship takes, it must go beyond a "Hi, how are you?" on Sunday morning. It must center in Jesus Christ, who is the very reason for it, and must show Christ's love to the world.

Paul's letters to the Corinthian church, a church struggling to hold its factious and sin-torn fellowship together, have much to teach us about the kind of Christian community God desires. It is a community that first of all recognizes a basic fact of its purpose and ministry in the world: it is the community of the King—called to be holy!

1
Mending Divisions

Truth to Apply: Knowing how God works through me and my church helps me bring unity rather than division.

Key Verse: I appeal to you, brothers, in the name of our Lord Jesus Christ, that all of you agree with one another so that there may be no divisions among you and that you may be perfectly united in mind and thought (I Cor. 1:10).

Perhaps no sport calls for more precise teamwork than rowing, especially for the eight-oared crew. Eight people sit in a sleek, shallow hull, their rowing motions synchronized by a coxswain. Far from being excess baggage, the coxswain calls out the cadence for each stroke, coordinating the efforts of the oarsmen. Each stroke from each side must occur at exactly the same time to maximize the efforts of the oarsmen and keep the boat on a straight, unwavering course. Without the coxswain, oarsmen soon would lose the coordination in their rowing, slowing down and perhaps coming to a stop, dead in the water. In an eight-oared rowing event, it's essential that eight people strive together as one to maximize the success of the team.

This striving together is also essential in the church. What happens to the Body of Christ when disunity is present? In what ways can church members work at overcoming divisions—to become a powerful unit, pulling together in one direction?

Paul wrote the first Letter to the Corinthians to respond to a letter he had previously received from the church. Specific answers to questions contained in their letter lie in chapters 7 to 15. But the first part of the letter addresses problems to which Paul was alerted by other sources. In this section, Paul responds to reports that the church at Corinth is suffering from a variety of divisions—at least four different factions.

The leaders of these factions probably had no intention of causing divisions in the church. The Corinthians just joined cliques that favored one style of leader over another. Paul's point was to show that Christians must rise above this trivial practice to present to the world a unified, Spirit-led witness.

The greeting in I Corinthians 1:1-3 follows a standard pattern for beginning letters in New Testament times. It contains three parts—the writer's name, the destination of the letter, and a greeting. Paul identifies himself as an "apostle" who has been called through the will of God. Apostle means "sent one." Paul received his call to apostleship on the road to Damascus and later was specifically sent by Christ as a missionary to the Gentiles (Acts 22:21).

Light on the Text

1:10, 11   Paul begins to discuss the problem of divisions, addressing the Corinthians twice as "brothers" and uses the verb "appeal." The rebuke shows his love for them and urges them to be bound by brotherly love, not split by divisions. Invoking the name of the Lord Jesus Christ increases the weight of his appeal. He asks them to agree, using a phrase typically employed to describe two hostile parties reaching an agreement. He wants them to be "perfectly united," the Greek word being a medical word used to describe the knitting together of bones that had been fractured or joining of a joint that had been dislocated. Paul uses the word *schismata* to describe the divisions, which is the word for gashes or tears in a garment.

1:12, 13 The church at Corinth had formed factions behind leaders or philosophies, and in doing so was acting without precedent and to the detriment of the church's witness. Christ wasn't divided in such a way—the Body of Christ was a unity. The leaders couldn't perform the work that Christ performed on the cross. The leaders only had power and relevance because they served God and pointed the way to Christ.

1:14-17 Paul notes that he baptized few of the Corinthians during his 18-month stay in the city, and he now sees that as providential. Because he baptized so few of them, it ruled out the possibility that he was binding converts to him and not to Christ. Paul's mission was not to lead a faction, but to tell others of Christ in simple terms, so that the full power of the Cross would be seen.

1:18-21 Paul begins to develop the contrast between worldly wisdom, which was so important to the Greeks, and the wisdom of God. Those who believe understand the true greatness and life-changing implication of the Gospel, while those who chose not to believe are blind to anything but the superficial.

The phrase "power of God" points to the fact that Paul is not merely sharing good advice or a message about God's power. It is God's power. The quotation from Isaiah 29:14 indicates that human wisdom, by itself, is bound to fail. It should place a person on a God-designed search that reveals his or her helplessness and need for Christ. Such a message, however, strikes many as foolish.

1:22-25 The Jews thought the Gospel was foolish for two reasons. First, they couldn't believe God's Chosen One would die on a cross in apparent conflict with Deut. 21:23. To the Jews, Jesus' death on the cross disproved

His deity. Second, the Jews sought signs. They expected the Messiah to come in a display of power. Jesus was meek and lowly, deliberately downplayed His miracles and took the form of a servant. The Greeks saw the Gospel as foolish because it presented God in human form and as suffering during His time on earth. Both contradicted their beliefs. Plutarch declared that it was an insult to God to involve Him in human affairs, and thus the very idea of the Incarnation was revolting. Also, the Greeks highly prized speculative philosophy and wisdom, specifically having a clever mind and a highly polished speaking method. To the Greeks, the Christian message seemed rather crude, blunt, and too black-and-white. The crucified Christ may appear to be the "weakness of God," but it is greater than the world's wisdom.

1:26-31 In verse 26, Paul reminds the Corinthians of their own condition before their calling. Not many were wise, but he chose them to shame those who thought they were wise. Not many were influential, but their weakness shamed the strong. Not many were of noble birth, but God chose them, lowly and despised. Because of God's initiative in choosing, and their lowliness, the possibility of boasting was excluded. They are in Christ, the closest possible relationship to Him.

In verse 30, Christ identifies four great things that Christ is for us. He is our wisdom, our righteousness, holiness, and redemption, which we could not have ever hoped to achieve on our own.

2:1-5 Paul's own presentation of the Gospel in Corinth was unadorned and thus may have appeared foolish in the eyes of the Greeks. But the effectiveness of his preaching among them served as a convincing demonstration of the power of God. Paul had shown the ability to argue in deep philosophical terms, as seen in his presentation of the Gospel on Mars' Hill (Acts 17:22-31). But in Corinth, Paul chose to focus on the crucified Christ. He came in weakness, in fear—with "anxiety to perform a duty"— and with much trembling. Despite the simplicity of the message, the results clearly demonstrated the power of the Spirit. The word translated "demonstration," signifies the most rigorous form of proof—in which the premises are known to be true and the conclusion is not only logical, but true.

For Discussion

1. What was the root cause of the Corinthian church's divisions? How can the solution Paul offered them help us avoid the same pitfall?

2. How willing are you to appear foolish for God? Share some examples of times in which you either avoided "looking foolish" as a Christian, or willingly allowed it.

3. At which basic human frailty does Paul hint in 1:29—2:5? In what situations is it difficult for you at times to restrain pride and give credit to God? How do you handle those situations?

4. What is Paul's initial teaching on the ministry of the Spirit? What difference does it make to your day-to-day life knowing you have a readily available source of intimate information about God? How have you been able to tap into this source?

Window on the Word

It is impossible to exaggerate the almost fantastic mastery that the silver-tongued rhetorician held in Greece. Plutarch says "They made their voices sweet with musical cadences and modulations of tone and echoed resonances." Their thought might be poisonous so long as it was enveloped in honeyed words. Philostratus tells us that Adrian, the sophist, had such a reputation in Rome, that when his messenger appeared with a notice that he was to lecture, the senate emptied and even the people at the games abandoned them to flock to hear him.

(William Barclay, *The Letters to the Corinthians*)

2

Seeking Spiritual Maturity

Truth to Apply: As I grow in spiritual maturity I can look away from myself to the well-being of others—and the growth of the church.

Key Verse: You are still worldly. For since there is jealousy and quarreling among you, are you not worldly? Are you not acting like mere men? (I Cor. 3:3).

As children grow up, they mature—but not always in the way we would think or prefer. Consider children's habits of playing with toys. Young infants often aren't aware of toys, but soon, they will learn to play for a short time with them. Even so, their attention span is short, and they don't particularly mind if another child takes their own toy away. That would seem to be a mature attitude, but it doesn't last long. By the time a child is one year old, he or she will protest loudly if a plaything is taken away. By two years of age, a child will fight to retain his or her right to a toy. From that age on, parents can never be sure—children may play together and gladly share any of their toys, or they may resort to full-scale war!

Unfortunately, the same responses can occur with adults. Angry responses can be elicited by almost anything. We show admirable maturity in one area, only to act like bickering three-year-olds in other areas. It can even happen in church when we fail to recognize our own pettiness.

How would you assess the general spiritual maturity level of your own group or church? What are your criteria?

Paul used several words to describe his relationship to the Corinthians. He calls himself an expert builder (3:10), who laid the foundation for their faith, the Gospel of Jesus Christ. He notes that because of his role in starting their church, he became their father (4:16), and addresses them both harshly and as "my dear children." Yet he realizes his God-given position—he is a servant of Christ, and also of the Corinthians, and a steward of the mysteries of God. This passage contains many contrasts of Paul's maturity with that of the Corinthians and shows how he puts his role into perspective. He wants to chide and lovingly direct his children so they attain the goal of spiritual maturity.

Light on the Text

3:1-4   Immediately after their conversion, the Corinthians were immature in their faith, and Paul doesn't appear to be finding fault with that. But that should change, and by Paul writing "Indeed, you are still not ready," he indicates their lack of a reasonable amount of spiritual development. The trouble is that the Corinthians were *sarkikoi*, which means not only made of flesh (literally), but dominated by the flesh or characterized by the mind-set that focuses on the fleshly things (spiritually). Christians were behaving like non-Christians. That is blameworthy; it is the very opposite of what a Christian should be. Their immaturity is expressed in their factions, which quarrel among themselves and give rise to jealousy. Thus, the Corinthians' actions were contrary to the spirit of the Gospel, and those actions damaged their witness to the world.

3:5-8   Asking the questions, "What, after all, is Apollos? And what is Paul?" emphasizes these leaders' functions, not their personality or style. Paul's point is that those admired by the factions are only servants, *diakonoi,* a word originally applied to the service of a table waiter. The word stresses the lowly character of the services rendered. Both one who plants the seed—Paul—and the one who waters—Apollos—are on the same level, and they don't have the power to actually *cause* spiritual growth to happen. Only God can do that, and the Greek verb form, in the imperfect, shows that God's activity is continous. The laborers are working for and in concert with God. The emphasis on God is driven home in verse 9, where three phrases emphasize God's centrality. The most accurate translation is that of the Authorized Version, which reads: "We are fellow-workers, and we both belong to God; you are God's husbandry; you are God's building." In a staggering turnabout, the Church is the subject of God's labor.

3:9-11 Continuing on the theme of building, Paul calls himself an expert builder. The position in ancient times reflected one who superintended the work of building. He asserts his unique position as the father of the Corinthian church, accomplished "by the grace God has given me." He recognized it was God's power alone that equipped him to do spiritual ministry. In verse 11, the phrase at the end is meant to dispel any doubt—the foundation is Jesus Christ, and no other. There is no proper religion without Jesus Christ. People can develop some degree of morality and spirituality on their own; but apart from Jesus Christ there is no salvation.

3:12-15 There are two types of works, the valuable (gold, silver, or costly stones) and the worthless (wood, hay or straw). Only workmanship and material of the highest quality are appropriate for God's temple, the Church.

Gold is the symbol of the costly, and may well represent the exercise of truth and holiness that will stand the test of Judgment Day. Silver is another metal which, like the results of our helpfulness to other Christians, will be purified and not destroyed by testing. I Peter 3:4 (RSV) speaks of "the imperishable jewel of a gentle and quiet spirit, which in God's sight is very precious." The combustible materials were used for the cheaper dwellings of Paul's day. Buildings made of these

17

materials were in constant danger of being destroyed by fire. We could take the wood, hay, and stubble to represent squabblings and the like, such as afflicted the Corinthians. The day of judgment will reveal their true nature and quickly remove them.

3:16, 17 It should be common knowledge to the Corinthians that believers are God's temple. In verse 16, the word temple is singular, but the "you" is plural. The word used here indicates the shrine proper, which points to the actual presence of God. The Church is the temple of God because it is the society in which the Spirit of God chooses to dwell. To defile means to profane or mar something. The temple of God, the Church, is holy; to defile it means to make it unholy. The preceding verses show that building bad material on the true foundation is equivalent to defiling God's temple. Using combustible material in God's temple mars its intended beauty, which would come if only gold, silver, and precious stones were used. Since the work of teachers is to teach doctrine, good building material would be true doctrine. Bad building material would be false doctrine.

3:18-20 The first hindrance to unity is inflated self-perceptions. The Corinthians are giving to themselves the glory God should be receiving. To see things from the world's viewpoint means to leave God out of the picture, to attempt to be independent of the Creator, to value things and people apart from a consideration of God's values. It is to look at time but not eternity.

3:21-23 The second hindrance to unity is the inflated perception of others. Paul writes this to emphasize that to divide into groups robs people of the benefits that could come from those outside their own group. The argument Paul presents here is that all people, and all things, are gifts from God. Offering themselves to His service, they become blessings to God's children. Because they have all things, Paul argues "Why do you limit yourself by following a particular teacher?" There was no limit to their possessions in Christ.

18

4:1-5 Ministers are servants, *huperetas*—a Greek word meaning those rowers who slaved in the lower bank of oars on a large ship. Ministers were stewards (KJV), entrusted with the secret things of God. In Paul's time, these stewards typically administered a master's estate and had authority over other slaves, but were subject to the master. Stewards will be judged on their faithfulness. They face judgment from others and from themselves, but the only judgment that finally matters is that of God, because only He can weigh secret deeds and motives.

4:6, 7 The Corinthians thought too highly of human leaders. "Taking pride" in one over another meant they were "against another." And finally, according to Paul, everything is a matter of grace: "What do you have that you did not receive?" In considering this verse, the fourth-century church father Augustine saw the whole doctrine of grace. He eventually said, "To solve this question, we labored hard in the cause of the freedom of man's will, but the grace of God won the day."

4:8-13 Paul contrasts the apostles' wretched lot and the comparative ease of the Corinthians' life-style. "You have all you want!" denotes satiation, a feeling of satisfaction. Comparatively, the Corinthians were well-fed, wealthy, and lived in an almost regal life-style. If that were truly the case, perhaps they could ease the life of the apostles. "The end of the procession" refers to the victorious return to Rome of a general—the last in the parade were the group of captives who were doomed to death. The idea is that God made them to be last. The apostles were "fools for Christ," while the Corinthians believed they had treasures of wisdom. The contrasts continue in verse 10, while verses 11-13 note the apostles' hardship, ending with the climax that they are the "refuse of the world," the vilest of the vile.

For Discussion

1. What are the causes of division in the church,

according to this passage? (See verses 3:3, 16-18; 4:5, 7.) How can we overcome these? (See verses 3:16; 4:1 and in relation to them, Phil. 2:5-11.)

2. What is Paul's perception of his role and proper spiritual attitude? How does it contrast with the Corinthians'?

3. How would you describe your own journey toward spiritual maturity up to the present time? Share some of the high points and low points. What have you learned about how God brings growth into our lives?

Window on the Word

A Great Prairie Fire

A Christian has only one foundation: Jesus Christ his Savior. And on that foundation he builds—with either combustible or noncombustible material. One day there will be a believers' judgment because we live in a moral universe and every book must be balanced in the presence of the holy Judge, and in the judgment the fire will come. I like to picture it as a great prairie fire which sweeps along burning everything in its path. Suddenly it comes to a great rock, leaps up over it and passes on. Everything on that rock which can be burned (the wood, hay and stubble) is consumed; everything that cannot be burned (the gold, silver and precious stones) stands for eternity. The Spirit inspired Paul to make it plain (and Paul knew the question would arise) that this does not concern salvation. The building may be destroyed but the builder still will live. The tragedy is that after we are born again, we can build upon the Rock things that are going to be consumed, so that after we have stood before the Lord Jesus Christ as Judge, we have little left. This is a danger not only to businessmen but to missionaries and ministers, not only to individuals but to congregations and organizations.

(Francis A. Schaeffer, *No Little People*, InterVarsity Press)

3

The Church's Holiness and Witness

Truth to Apply: My moral purity and my ability to get along with other Christians is a powerful witness to those around me.

Key Verse: Do you not know that your body is a temple of the Holy Spirit . . . ? (I Cor. 6:19)

It was a story of sexual immorality, litigation, charges, countercharges. A woman who was a member of a church in the South was accused of sexual immorality, and the church's board decided to have her excommunicated so she no longer could attend the church. Rather than accepting their judgment, the woman went to the courts and filed a lawsuit.

Soon, every bit of "dirty laundry" concerning the woman was out in public view. She, in turn, based much of her defense on the basis that the church was hypocritical in its action—its members weren't without sin, and she attempted to reveal every bit of immorality she could find about other church members.

All the while, newspapers across the country found out about the story and printed long accounts or sordid details almost daily.

Our indiscretions may not receive as much publicity, but the cumulative effect of them is the same. How do our shortcomings hurt the witness of both the Universal Church and the local church? What is your experience with trying to "witness" (or be witnessed to) in word only?

Corinth was located on a narrow isthmus between the Aegean and Adriatic seas. It was a port city and wealthy commercial center. It was the site of much traffic because boat captains that wanted to avoid the dangerous trip around the southern tip of Greece had their ships dragged across the isthmus. Besides the influx of merchants and their wealth, Corinth also was the site of the Isthmian games, second only to the Olympics in popularity.

Corinth, however, also was a city enmeshed in immoral living. A Greek word, *korinthiazomai,* was a derivative of "Corinthian," and it meant to act like a Corinthian, to practice immorality or whoredom—it was synonymous with debauchery. Near the city was the hill of the Acropolis, and it was the site of the temple of Aphrodite, the goddess of love. It contained 1,000 prostitutes. This was the society from which members of the Corinthian church came and in which it struggled to achieve spiritual purity.

Light on the Text

5:1-5 A man in the church reportedly had sexual relations with his father's wife (although the exact meaning isn't clear, it possibly refers to a stepmother divorced from the father). Even more shocking, the church had allowed the situation to continue without taking action—instead, they were proud, perhaps indicating they believed they were taking an enlightened approach. Rather, they should have been mourning, exhibiting a grief that they normally would show for the dead. For punishment, Paul specifies excommunication. It was discipline exercised with the intention of causing the sinner to awaken and repent so the "spirit [may be] saved on the day of the Lord."

5:6-8   Paul again addresses the Corinthians' attitude. They did more than tolerate sexual impropriety; they were proud of their permissive attitude. He then turns to an Old Testament illustration to show the danger in which their attitude placed the church. The word translated "yeast" refers to the leaven—dough left over from a previous baking that had fermented and was sour the next day. The Jews contrasted fermentation with purification, and leaven was considered a corrupting influence. Before the Passover festival, the Jews ceremoniously searched their houses for leaven to discard it before sacrificing their lamb or kid goat for the Passover sacrifice. For seven days before the sacrifice, the Jews ate unleavened bread. Paul brings this to mind now, urging the Corinthians to "get rid of the old yeast that you may be a new batch without yeast, as you really are." The new batch produces bread of sincerity, or purity of motive; and truth, or purity of action. If the leaven is bad, the whole lump of dough will be sour. What holds for dough also holds for a community. The Corinthians must take drastic action in expelling the offender because of the peril of his influence.

5:9-13   Paul already has written to the church at Corinth, urging them to avoid the society of all evil people. He meant that to apply to members of the church: wicked people must be put out of the church until they have changed their ways. But the Corinthians misunderstood. They took Paul's admonition to mean that they should avoid all contact with unbelievers, which of course would mean, especially in a city like Corinth, that they would have to withdraw from the world altogether. Christians should not avoid contact with non-Christians, but they can stop associating with any professing Christian whose life is a reproach to everything the church should represent to the community.

    Paul lists several sins which are typical of the world (vss. 10, 11), cautioning the Corinthians against allowing these sins to exist in the church.

    Christians are not, however, to judge those outside the Church. they must leave that judgment to God, for He alone knows the heart of every person. But those within the Church have special privileges as children of God and therefore have important responsibilities as well. They are responsible to answer to Him for the way they handle those responsibilities.

6:1-3 The Corinthians had been taking one another into the public courts to settle disputes. The Greek culture in general enjoyed the spectacle of litigation. To them, the courts were a colorful source of entertainment. They had a legal process that involved many citizens. In Greece, a legal dispute first was brought before an arbitrator or a panel of three arbitrators. If no settlement was reached, the dispute went to a court known as The Forty, which assigned the matter to public arbitrators. If the matter still was unsettled, it went to a jury court that could involve as few as 201 jurors for smaller cases or as many as 6,000 for major cases. Thus, in a Greek city, every man spent much time either deciding or listening to law cases.

6:4-6 One reason Paul gives for Christians not taking one another to law may sound startling and mysterious to our ears: the saints are destined to judge the world (vs. 2) and angels (vs. 3). Are they not then fit to settle disputes among themselves?

The meaning of verse 4 is not certain. "Therefore, if you have disputes about such matters, appoint as judges even men of little account in the church!" But another possible translation of the Greek words turns the statement into a question: "Do you appoint as judges men of little account in the church?" The Living Bible paraphrases the verse this way: "Why then go to outside judges who are not even Christians?"; then footnotes, "Even the least capable people in the church should be able to decide these things for you."

Obviously, from Paul's comments at the beginning of this letter, it was apparent the Corinthians took pride in their wisdom. Now, he chides them by wondering if they can't find even one wise person among them to give a decision.

6:7, 8   Paul's Christian principles make the thought of two
feuding Christians going to law in a public court
revolting to him. How can a Christian look for justice in
the presence of the unjust?

The essential principle is this: To go to law with a
Christian brother or sister is to fall far below Christ's
standard. Christians should live at peace with fellow
Christians and refrain from seeking to gain an advantage
over them.

The highest and final reason for settling grievances
peaceably, without resort to public courts of law, is the
teaching and example of Jesus: Christians should always
be willing to *suffer wrong* rather than *do wrong*.

6:9-11   The Corinthians have received a lofty calling, saved from
lives that couldn't possibly merit any fate other than
condemnation by God.

Paul's list of sinners includes those who sin against
themselves by practicing sexual vice and those who sin
against others. These couldn't expect to inherit, or enter
into the full possession of God's Kingdom. But the
Corinthian believers, who had practiced these sins before
their conversion, could expect that inheritance because
of the washing away of sins in Christ through
sanctification, or God's making them distinctively His
own; and through justification, so that they are now
pronounced righteous in Christ. This miraculous
deliverance to bountiful reward should cause believers to
live lives dedicated to obedience to God.

For Discussion

1. In Paul's opinion, how important was it to keep the
church morally pure? Is it easy for churches today to
slide toward the lax position of the church at Corinth?
Why?

2. In what ways could your own church body begin to
apply verse 6:4? Would you apply it literally?

3. What general principal for solving disputes among
Christians do you see in 6:1-8?

4. How would you act differently if you were continually aware that God's Spirit is indwelling you? Name some ways you could try to "practice His presence" this week.

Window on the Word

Together Again

The Greeks had a legend that men and women were once joined together in pairs, and that the gods in a playful moment divided and separated them. It is in love and marriage that men and women rediscover one another and are reunited. That is actually what happily married people feel about one another. As they share time and experiences with the one they love, as they embrace and fellowship with one another emotionally, intellectually, spiritually, and physically, it is as if the deep ache of their hearts is ended and the open wound caused by their severance from one another is healed at last.

(David R. Mace, *Whom God Hath Joined*, Westminster)

4

Marriage and Service to God

Truth to Apply: When I consider major decisions, such as marriage, I must first take into account the implications it will have on my relationship with, and service to, God.

Key Verse: I am saying this for your own good, not to restrict you, but that you may live in a right way in undivided devotion to the Lord (I Cor. 7:35).

Jim Elliot was one of five missionaries killed by the Auca Indians in 1956. His life of devotion to Christ has been well documented by his wife, Elizabeth. In her book, *Shadow of the Almighty,* she recalls how Jim struggled with the decision to marry. He was concerned with the impact such a decision would have on his ability to serve God.

At age 23, he showed his dilemma in a letter to his parents. "I cannot condition myself to think of marriage now, in spite of all the rings and bells, not to mention the abundance of marriageable women on the horizon . . . I do not feel it fair, either to the girl or to the work of the Lord, to tie myself up right now with all that a relationship involves . . . ."

Although he long believed he would be an unmarried missionary, Jim eventually came to believe that marriage to Elizabeth was a part of God's will and harmonious with his plans for missionary service. A letter to his parents said, "I think I have the will of God in this."

How much "say" does God have in determining the direction of our lives? How do you, personally, go about deciding what is God's will?

In chapters 7—15 Paul begins to respond to specific questions the Corinthian church had apparently posed to him in a previous letter. Paul didn't intend to write a treatise on marriage in chapter 7; he simply is responding to various specific questions asked of him. The questions are prompted by the different cultures represented in the church at Corinth and their approaches to marriage.

Three facts can help us understand the nature of Paul's responses to these questions:

1) Paul answered the questions based on the underlying belief that Christ's return was likely to occur at any time. Paul was probably giving advice on an empending distress known to the Corinthians.

2) The church at Corinth was located in one of the most immoral settings in the world. It's natural that Paul would emphasize strictness rather than laxity in his answers.

3) Although Paul seemed to advocate celibacy, he regards marriage as normal and offering greater completeness. In Ephesians, Paul says marriage offers a glimpse of the relationship of Christ to the Church.

Light on the Text

7:1, 2 Commentators have different opinions on what specific questions of the Corinthians Paul was attempting to answer. Because of this, there are a variety of opinions on how the chapter should be divided.

In the early centuries, many admired an ascetic way of life, and celibacy was one of those admired ascetic practices. In Greek thought, there was a tendency to despise the body, considering the "spiritual" to be the only important concern. Though for some this meant complete freedom to do anything with the body that one wanted to do, others came to the opposite conclusion: all the instincts and desires of the body must be suppressed. But Paul refuses to be placed exclusively in either camp. The body must be respected and valued as God's creation. To ignore it is to ignore God's work. But to indulge it frivolously is to ignore one's moral responsibilities.

Paul begins by saying that "it is good for a man not to marry" because the single person is better able to serve God. But the immorality of Corinth leads him to command marriage, except in certain cases (vs. 7). In these verses, Paul indicates that the desire to retain purity should play a role in making the decision about marriage (vs. 2).

7:3-7 Some members of the church at Corinth apparently reasoned that if a Christian wanted to be spiritual, he or she must abandon physical things entirely. For example, a man must either refuse to marry or, if already married, must himself forego and deny his spouse the physical intimacies associated with marriage.

The notion that a superior spiritual love would not require physical intimacy actually results from a concept of the body as something inferior, a vehicle of sin rather than of grace. But if sex within marriage is a gift of God and the body a sacred vessel to be given back to Him, then a superior love does not deny physical expression. Only an inferior kind of love is unwilling to take seriously the needs of the partner, thus rejecting God's gift of sexuality. Both husband and wife have a right to the physical fulfillment of their love.

Paul suggests in verse 6, however, that verses 3-5 represent not an ideal command, but a concession to human needs. His personal preference would be for everyone to be as he himself is. Paul does not downgrade marriage; he only insists that every Christian should be devoted to Christ. Paul declares his personal preference for a life of celibacy if that life can be free from restlessness and dissatisfaction. Each individual, however, is free to act according to his or her personal circumstances. The capacity for single living is a special gift, and those who do not possess this gift should marry.

Paul suggests our decisions should be made in light of the type and extent of action it will require (vs. 3); the affects of our decision on others, especially if it will cause them to sin (vs. 5c); and the gifts the individual possesses (vs. 7).

7:8, 9   Paul mentions the unmarried, which includes all not bound in marriage. In addition, he makes special mention of the widows. The phrase "I say" denotes his opinion, which is that, if possible, it's good for them to remain unmarried. However, there is no advantage to clinging to celibacy if a person is consumed with passion and can't control it. In those cases, Paul urges marriage.

7:10, 11   In verses 10-16, Paul responds to a series of situations regarding divorce. In marriages where both partners are Christians, he has an authoritative command from Jesus Himself—they are not to divorce. If they do, they must remain unmarried or reconcile.

    The factor in making a decision here is whether there is a direct command from God in the Bible on the matter.

7:12-16   Paul now addresses the cases in which a believer is married to an unbeliever. He's responding to a belief in Corinth that believers shouldn't remain married to unbelievers. Adherence to this caused the breakup of many families in the first century. In this case, Paul offers his opinion, although he considers it authoritative. The marriage should be maintained, but much depends on the attitude of the unbelieving partner—if he or she desires that the marriage continue, it should be continued. If not, the believer isn't constrained from marrying again (according to one interpretation). The underlying principle should be one of promoting peace.

    There are two benefits of continuing the marriage, Paul notes. The unbelieving family is consecrated (under the sanctifying *influence* of) by the believer—the blessings, to some extent, reach to the unbelievers. And the believer may be the means God uses to cause the unbeliever to repent. However, verse 16 implies that this is never a sure result, only a possibility.

    These verses show that our witness, with the intent of extending sanctification to others, can help us make decisions.

7:17-24 Here Paul broadens the principle to include forbearance in all situations. He refers directly to circumcision and slavery, large religious and social distinctions in his day. Normal practice for believers is remaining in their present states, in which God has assigned, called and, ostensibly, empowered a believer to live. Jewish Christians were likely to insist on circumcision, but in Christ, the distinction between circumcision and uncircumcision does not matter. One who is a slave shouldn't worry about his or her status. The goal is to make the old life new because of the influence of Christ as the Christian's new "owner."

Paul makes the point that slaves are freed and have been elevated because of Christ's sacrifice; those who are free, through the same sacrifice, have been called to be Christ's slave. Bought at the price of Christ's blood, Christians are not to return to be the slaves of others. Believers should be content in the situations in which they find themselves.

Concerning guidance, these verses show that God's will involves specific callings (vs. 17a); God will call the Christian to that place (vs. 17b); God's commands overshadow all other factors (vs. 19); and because of Christ's sacrifice, we can trust God and are responsible to God.

7:25 Paul begins to answer a question about virgins, but the specific answer doesn't appear until verses 36-38. His comments in verses 26-35 reveal the rationale behind his answers.

Here Paul notes that he is going to give his opinion, not a command from God. How do we understand this to be both Paul's opinion and the Word of God? According to the NIV Study Bible (Zondervan): "Paul is not giving a direct command from Jesus here (as in v. 10; cf Ac 20:35). In this matter, which is not a question of right and wrong, Paul expresses his own judgment. Even though he put it this way, he is certainly not denying that he wrote under the influence of divine inspiration (see v. 40). And since he writes under inspiration, what he recommends is clearly the better course of action." This points to the importance of the advice of others, especially those wiser and more mature, in trying to make an appropriate decision.

7:26-31 The basis for Paul's advice is a present crisis—or distress, as other versions say. It's not clear what the problem was, but the word is a strong one. The full impact of the crisis will result in great changes, as listed in verses 29-31. Christians shouldn't be totally occupied with the things of the world. The focus should be on eternal things. Paul's advice is that in the troubled times the Corinthians were to experience, it's best not to attempt drastic, stressful changes.

7:32-35 The difficulty of marriage is manifested by the split in allegiance that it causes. Such a relationship inevitably and understandably will distract from service to God. The distraction is natural for both men and women— marriage introduces an entire new set of concerns, including service to and pleasing the spouse.

Paul's goal of devotion to God, stated in verse 35, should form the foundational cornerstone for a decision-making philosophy.

7:36-38 Paul returns to the subject of virgins. However, there is confusion about to whom Paul refers in this portion. Two main theories have been offered: 1) The man is the parent or guardian of the girl, and the passage refers to arranging a marriage for her; 2) The subjects are a man and his fiancée. There are reasons for and against all three interpretations. The verb indicating the action of the man in verse 39, "gives away," is the Greek word *gamizo,* which isn't in reference to brides. Verse 38 indicates the man has the authority to do what he wills.

Many commentators lean toward the first interpretation. In any case, the instruction of Paul is consistent. Celibacy offers the best opportunity to serve God, but the option of marriage is acceptable.

7:39, 40 In giving advice for widows, Paul also remains consistent. If her husband dies, she can remarry anyone as long as that person is a Christian. Here, Paul's rationale is only that the widow will be happier if she remains single after the death of her husband.

For Discussion

1. What overriding concerns should we have, whether we are married or single?

2. In your opinion, what are the most important principles in this chapter for making a major decision? Which is the most sacrificial for you?

3. Describe how you have made a tough decision in the past? How did you do it? What happened? What would you do differently if you could relive the experience? Why?

4. How do you apply 7:24 to your own life? Should we never try to change our jobs, gain professional advancement, move to a new house? Explain.

Window on the Word

Paul's Own Marital Status

Many scholars believe Acts 26:10 shows Paul was a member of the Sanhedrin and therefore must have been married. Jewish regulations required members of the Sanhedrin to be married men. Marriage was considered an obligation of anyone who would claim to be an orthodox Jew. However, the Bible makes no direct mention of Paul having a wife. Paul's mention in I Cor. 9:5 that he did not make use of his right to bring along a wife on his journeys seems to confirm that Paul was single when he wrote this letter.

What happened to Paul's wife? Perhaps she died. Other scholars believe it's possible she left him after his conversion. If so, Paul could rightfully say that he gave up everything for the sake of Christ.

5

Christian Liberty: Use and Abuse

Truth to Apply: I must be willing to limit my freedom in Christ when it might cause other believers to stumble or when it would hurt the witness of the church.

Key Verse: So whether you eat or drink or whatever you do, do it all for the glory of God. Do not cause anyone to stumble, whether Jews, Greeks or the church of God (I Cor. 10:31, 32).

There are many adjustments to make when you move to a rural town from a big city. When one Chicago resident moved to a small rural Illinois town, she was most impressed by the courtesy of the drivers. Perhaps impressed isn't the right word—she was amazed, especially when it came to using the crosswalk on the town's main street. A sign advised drivers to stop for pedestrians, and believe it or not, they actually obeyed it!

Within a few months, she became accustomed to enjoying the freedom of stepping boldly into the crosswalk, striding out into the street and having all cars immediately stop. Then she moved back to Chicago. As a pedestrian walking downtown, she remembered that exercising that same freedom was hazardous to her health. While the city had similar rules about yielding to pedestrians as the little town did, it seemed as though most drivers believed it was open season on pedestrians.

While Christians have received freedom through Christ's death, there are times we must limit it for our sake and out of regard for others. What are those instances? What guidelines can help us decide when to restrict our freedom?

In addition to questions about marriage, another item of concern about which the Corinthians wrote to Paul was the issue of whether they could eat meat offered to idols. Worshippers of an idol would bring a sacrifice as an offering, but usually only a token amount of the offering was burned on the altar. Part of the sacrifice would be taken by the priests of the temple; some was taken to be sold to the general public at a shop outside the temple; and the rest would be returned to the worshiper, who often would use it as the main course of a meal at the temple. He would invite friends to join in the meal, which often would include much laughter, song, and drunken revelry. In this way, it was a social occasion as well as a quasi-religious experience.

The Corinthians wondered if it was correct to eat meat purchased from the shops since it was very likely that the portions had been cut from animals sacrificed and dedicated to idols. They also questioned whether it was acceptable to participate in the meals at the temples of idols if they were invited.

Light on the Text

8:1-3   Before discussing the dilemma of whether to eat meat offered to idols, Paul first discusses what undoubtedly was the basis for the Corinthians' thinking. True, all people possess knowledge, but it has its shortcomings, not the least of which is the pride it can foster. Earthly knowledge is partial and incomplete. Love, on the other hand, edifies. God responds to a person who loves Him by *knowing* that person.

8:4-6   On the question at hand, Paul refers to what is known—an idol, as a representation of a god, as nothing because the gods the heathen worship aren't really gods. Rather, there is only one God (Deut. 6:4). Verse 6 repeats the thought for both God the Father and the Lord Jesus Christ, attributing to the only true God the creation and sustenance of the universe. The focus is on Christianity's monotheism and the deity of Christ.

8:7, 8   While this knowledge existed, it was not universal. Some of the new converts at the Corinthian church had grown up in the pagan culture and had worshiped idols. They were so accustomed to believing that the idol was real that they thought they were doing wrong by eating meat that had been offered to idols. Food is not an important enough point to inflict this guilt on those who felt this way.

8:9-13   The principle is expanded—a Christian believer shouldn't exercise his or her rightful freedom if it causes harm to another. A stumbling block, *proskomma,* is a stone in the path that trips a traveler up and makes progress difficult. Verse 10 takes the form of a rhetorical question—someone with a weak conscience will not be emboldened to eat food offered to idols. They will be destroyed by the action of those who have "knowledge" (or freedom). This is particularly bad, because the person who is being destroyed is one for whom Christ died. As such, the sin against weak brothers or sisters through wounding (striking blows) their conscience is also a sin against Christ! Shifting to a first-person treatment in verse 13, Paul says he avoids any practice that would cause a brother to fall into sin.

9:1-3   In this chapter, Paul gives the Corinthians examples of ways in which he has limited privileges due him so that they would not be a stumbling block to others as he performs his ministry. He shows that he has the right to claim privileges since he is an apostle, having seen Jesus on the road to Damascus.

   The blessing of God has been on his work because of the effectiveness of his ministry, as seen in the Corinthians themselves. They were his seal. In those days, a seal, stamped on clay or wax, was an official mark of ownership and authenticity. This is an effective defense to all who would be critics of Paul.

9:4-18 Should Paul claim support, it would only be reasonable. Soldiers don't serve at their own expense—they receive provisions; the farmer who plants a vineyard shares in the fruit; the shepherd gets his food from the flock.

Even the Law of Moses (Deut. 25:4) notes that the oxen that work the threshing machine are not to be muzzled, but allowed to eat of the harvested grain, and this is expanded by Paul to include those in Christian service. Spiritual labor is performed with the understanding that material payment will be received (vs. 11). Those who work in the Temple and serve at the altar share in the offerings (vs. 13). And an unrecorded saying of the Lord, perhaps something similar to Luke 10:7, notes that those that preach the Gospel should receive wages for their labor (vs. 14). But Paul did not exercise the right to support, hoping to eliminate the chance that doing so would "hinder the gospel."

Paul didn't intend to seek support from the church at Corinth. He cannot boast in this because he is "compelled to preach," a duty befitting God's special grace to him. His reference to a reward perhaps relates to I Cor. 3:14. To preach without support *was* Paul's reward—a gracious privilege!

9:19-23 Paul surrendered much of his liberty in adopting his philosophy of ministry. He was a free man and a Roman citizen, but these he surrendered so that he might be a "slave to everyone" to win them to Christ. Paul, though no longer bound to the law of the Jews, respected their beliefs and conformed to their practices so he could approach them. He also related to those "not having the law"—the Gentiles—within limits, in efforts to win them. To the weak, he became weak. In summary, Paul had surrendered claims to all of his liberties so that he could become all things to all people in hopes of gaining a hearing from as many as possible.

9:24-27 In addition to surrendering rights and freedoms, Paul's ministry involved dedication, self-control, and effort similar to that of an athlete in the Isthmian Games who has a very definite aim and is concentrating on the prize. Christians similarly must exert every effort. "Competes in the games" is the verb *agonizomai*, from which we derive the word "agonize," and it shows a halfhearted effort is not good enough. The prize for such extended training is a wreath of leaves that lasts only a few days. By contrast, Christians will receive a crown that lasts forever. The eternal prize carries with it an equal responsibility, and it makes Paul purposeful. He doesn't "run" aimlessly, because he knows where the finish line is. He doesn't aim punches at the air, because a real enemy exists. He disciplines himself so he won't be disqualified for the prize (I Cor. 3:15).

10:14-22 From seeing the example God made of the Israelites, Paul urges the Corinthians to flee from idolatry. The word "flee" is a verb tense that connotes habitual practice, meaning the Corinthians are to constantly be on guard. Paul then emphasizes the participation inherent in both the Lord's Supper and idol worship. The word participation is koinonia, or communion or fellowship. Through the cup and the breaking of bread, we enter into close communion with Jesus and with each other, creating unity in both instances. Whether an idol is real is inconsequential; Paul believes demons make use of the idols to distract persons from God, and thus a sacrifice to an idol is, by extension, a sacrifice to demons. Christians cannot enter into fellowship with demons in this way, because no one can enter into close fellowship with both the spiritual adversaries of darkness and light. One necessarily must exclude the other. To continue in the current practice is to "fellowship" with demons and risk the response of the Lord's jealousy.

10:23-30 While Christian liberty set a person free to do all things, not all things are wise. They may not benefit the person doing them or the brothers and sisters who see them doing it. In the Corinthians' specific situation, Paul says they should be most concerned with the good of others and not merely practice their own liberty. They can eat meat sold in the meat market—which may have contained meat from the temples—without questioning their conscience. A believer can participate in a dinner at a private home, unless the guest notes specifically that the meat came from an offering to an idol. Then, a believer was not to eat it to make sure not to offend the other believer's conscience.

10:31-33 This section contains three principles to guide us:
1. Put the good of others first, ahead of your own. Paul says that we ought to seek not our own profit but the profit of others in order that they might be saved (vs. 33).
2. Do all to the glory of God (vs. 31), constantly asking ourselves if an action brings credit to Christ.
3. Try to offend (i.e., cause damage to) no one, either outside or inside the church (vs. 32).

For Discussion

1. What situations or activities do Christians disagree about as to whether they are permissible Christian behavior? What guidelines can we call on?

2. We generally don't like to have our freedoms restricted in "gray areas." What can Paul's example teach us?

3. What warning can we derive from the experience of the Israelites? How does it apply specifically to us?

4. What is your own experience in dealing with a "weaker" brother or sister?

Window on the Word

At a feast in an idol temple, it was always held that the god himself was a guest. More, it was often held that after the meat had been sacrificed, the god himself was in it and that at the banquet he entered into the very bodies and spirits of those who ate. Just as an unbreakable bond was forged between two men if they ate each other's bread and salt, so a sacrificial meal formed a real communion between the god and his worshipper. The person who sacrificed in a real sense was a sharer with the altar; he had a mystic communion with the god.
(William Barclay, *The Letters to the Corinthians*)

6

The Importance Of Proper Worship

Truth to Apply: I must cultivate the proper attitude for worship, having a focus on Christ, ready to emulate His example of service.

Key Verse: For whenever you eat this bread and drink this cup, you proclaim the Lord's death until he comes (I Cor. 11:26).

On his radio show "Chapel of the Air," David Mains stresses the point that most people today don't give any thought to preparing for worship. It's true—unless we have a specific duty to fulfill during our hours at church, we generally give no thought to worship time until Sunday. Unfortunately, even on Sunday, more often than not, we're merely thinking about the logistics of getting to church on time. When we are there and finally have some quiet moments to think, it's easy for our minds to stray, perhaps by talking to other people there, perhaps by compiling mental lists of things we have to do during the remainder of the day. When we get home, it's no wonder we can't even recall the topic of the sermon! In contrast to this, Mains has urged the investment of time and effort to prepare for worship. His suggestions range from selecting Sunday clothes in advance to spending advance time thinking about what we expect to get out of the worship service. Worship succeeds in praising God when we are spiritually and mentally cleansed and focused on our role.

What things can distract you on Sunday mornings? In what ways would you like your worship experience to become more meaningful?

The church in Corinth was having its worship services disrupted by at least two peculiarities. Verses 2-16 show Paul's reaction to the fact that women in the church had decided—probably because of their newfound Christian liberty—not to wear their veils during public worshsip. But in the East in Paul's time, women wore a veil that only left the eyes exposed, and a respectable woman would never appear in public without it. Without the veil, a woman of that time would be suspected of having loose morals.

The Corinthians were also suffering from divisions because of problems associated with a fellowship meal that preceded the Lord's Supper. Called the Agape, or Love Feast, it came to represent the unity and bond of love among the members of the church. All members of the church, whether rich or poor, brought what they could to the feast. The poor were not able to bring much—indeed, the meal at the Love Feast was probably their best of the week. But in Corinth, the rich made a mockery of the meal—some of the wealthier members arrived early and greedily ate their food and drank so much that they were intoxicated when the poor, mostly slaves, arrived. In many ways, this jaded feast had superseded the Lord's Supper in importance and was a poor witness.

Light on the Text

11:2   Paul begins this section by praising the Corinthians for the way they had adhered to the traditions he had handed down to them. Perhaps he is even referring to aspects of the worship service and the Lord's Supper. There is the hint that Paul hopes these words similarly will be taken to heart and followed.

11:3-6   Paul develops a strong position on the matter of whether Christian women should wear veils in public worship at the Corinthian church. For Christian men, it had become an accepted practice for them to pray with their heads uncovered—it was a dishonor to pray otherwise. For the Christian woman, it was viewed as a dishonor to her if she prayed or prophesied *without* her head covered. It was a disgrace equal to having her head shaved!

11:7-10 A man need not cover his head because he is made in the image and glory of God (Gen. 1:26, 27). The woman, on the other hand, was made from the man, and she is the glory of man. Paul notes that originally the woman was created from and for the man. For this reason, a woman should wear a veil—it is her symbol that secures for her a position of dignity and authority. With it, she can act properly before the angels, which are present at all times but especially at worship services.

11:11, 12 Paul is quick to assure that women are more than just property for men to control. Neither the man nor woman are independent but *interdependent*. This is because they both are involved in an aspect of creation.

11:13-16 Paul tries to use reason, especially as it applies to the customs of the day for hair length. Because it was the custom for most men to have short hair, it was a disgrace to have long hair in the case of men. Women's long hair indicated the need for a covering—for a woman, unlike a man, long hair was "her glory." In any case, the point was not open for discussion, as far as Paul was concerned. That women wear a veil was the practice at other Christian churches.

Churches debate how appropriate it is to apply the ruling of Paul in these matters at Corinth to churches of the 20th century. However, the verses do show us that we need to accept faithfully the fact that God has ordained a certain order of stewardship. In addition, it appears that our liberty under Christ is limited—our freedom stops when it destroys the witness of the church.

11:17-19 In the next matter, Paul has no praise for the Corinthians. The Lord's Supper, intended to be the most edifying of worship services, instead had become an occasion in which more harm was done than good.

Instead of unity, the Communion service caused divisions (*schismata,* the same Greek word used in I Cor. 1:10). Paul sarcastically suggests that the factions thrive because their members are arguing about who has God's favor. Instead, they merit God's anger because their actions subvert the work of the church.

11:20-22

Verse 20 notes the misdirected intentions of the Corinthians—the abused Love Feast has overshadowed the Lord's Supper—and hints that their celebration no longer resembles the celebration instituted by Christ.

Paul describes what he has heard, that the rich arrive early at the love feast, hungry and anxious to eat, and that they proceed with the food and drink before others arrive. It's likely that slaves would not be able to bring much food and would have the day's tasks to complete before they could attend the meal and Lord's Supper. While they remained hungry, the early arrivers had overindulged, as indicated by the use of the word drunk. This action showed a lack of love for the church and was humiliating to the poor. Paul directs them to eat at home if they cannot keep themselves under control.

11:23-26

The tradition of the Lord's Supper was received by Paul, and he is passing it on to the Corinthians. This letter, written about 55 A.D., was written earlier than any of the Gospels, and thus it formed the earliest record of the first Communion. Through the simple, common actions of taking, giving thanks for and breaking ordinary bread, Jesus announces the turning point in the world's history—Himself.

The breaking of bread is always to be a remembrance of His coming. The cup containing the fruit of the vine is the cup of "the new covenant." Jesus' death on the cross for all people forever would change the relationship between humankind and God. This new agreement or covenant means God will view as righteous all who repent and accept Christ's sacrifice for themselves. The remembrance provoked by the Communion service is meant to be a witness to Christ's death and resurrection until He returns to claim the people of the New Covenant, who now are God's people.

11:27-34 Leon Morris, commenting on verse 27, writes, "There is a sense in which all must partake *unworthily*, for none can ever be worthy of the goodness of Christ to us. But in another sense we can come worthily, i.e., in faith, and with a due performance of all that is fitting for so solemn a rite. To neglect this is to come *unworthily*. A man who does this is *guilty of the body and blood of the Lord.* The greatness of the gift that is offered is the measure of the greatness of his guilt." Some commentators have suggested that Paul also means that we must not come without proper love, respect, and service toward other Christians—the Body of Christ, the Church. F. W. Grosheide offers this helpful explanation of verse 29: "They who abuse the Holy Supper cause the judgment of God to come upon them. To recognize means to determine the value of the Communion by regarding it as something different. By not coming to the table in the right manner, one does not regard the body (i.e., the body and the blood) as it should be regarded." God's judgments include the fact that Paul says that some of the Corinthians were sick or had died because of partaking unworthily.

For Discussion

1. What is Paul's main point in verses 2-16? What is achieved by illustrating subjection to God in this way?

2. From this passage, it appears the Lord's Supper is meant to exemplify Christian unity, and be a witness to Christ's resurrection until He comes back. Does the service at your church accomplish these goals? How could you emphasize one of these goals at the next Communion service?

3. A critical part of any Communion service is self-examination. Is this a part of your personal preparation for Communion? In what two ways could you prepare before Communion to receive the bread and the cup more worthily?

4. Share your most meaningful time of worship. What

made it so meaningful? How could such an experience be repeated in the worship services of your church?

Window on the Word

It is important to realize the continuity between the Lord's Supper, the central observance of the New Covenant, and the Passover, the most important observance of the Old Covenant. Down through the centuries, the Passover was faithfully observed: by Moses at Sinai (Num. 9:5), by Joshua in Canaan (Josh. 5:10), by King Hezekiah after the captivity of Israel (II Chr. 30:13), by Josiah before Judah's captivity (II Ki. 23:21), and by all the people who returned from captivity (Ezra 6:19). That Jesus kept the Passover can be seen in Matthew 26:19; Mark 14:12; Luke 22:7; and John 13.

The Holy Spirit revealed to Paul that the Passover was a type, or foreshadowing, of Christ's death (I Cor. 5:7).

It is likely that the early Christians followed the familiar Passover custom of singing the "Egyptian Hallel," Psalms 113—118. Perhaps this is the meaning of Mark 14:26, "When they had sung a hymn, they went out to the Mount of Olives."

(*New Bible Dictionary*)

7

Using Spiritual Gifts

Truth to Apply: I am called to use my spiritual gifts to strengthen and edify others in the church.

Key Verse: Since you are eager to have spiritual gifts, try to excel in gifts that build up the church (I Cor. 14:12).

Unfortunately, giving or receiving gifts isn't always a pleasurable experience. It's sad, but the day after Christmas can be a time for much second-guessing and unkind thoughts. Some responses may sound like this: "Why did Mary get me that shirt?" "Where would I wear something that's purple with orange stripes?" "The folks must have spent three times as much on my brother as they did on me. I would have rather received something like they gave John." "I asked for bathroom appliances and accessories, so they got me a Mount Rushmore toothbrush holder. How am I going to take that back?"

Not getting what we want, not getting "enough" or high enough quality—these are all responses that can be traced back to our pride. That same trait can do much to negate the spiritual gifts we receive. Thus we hinder, rather than help, spiritual growth in the church. In what ways are you presently using a spiritual gift or talent to strengthen your local church?

According to the ancient religious culture, those who were in close touch with the gods would exhibit special spiritual manifestations—trances, ecstatic speech, or other similar mystical phenomena. To many early believers, speaking in tongues was the best way to exhibit high spirituality. Some regarded themselves as more important, others were jealous, and others simply withdrew from involvement. Paul points to the necessity for unity under Christ's headship, the importance of all gifts, and love as the greatest gift that sets the standard for exercising all others.

The Corinthian church seemed to have been blessed with an abundance of spiritual gifts, yet instead of being drawn together by them, they were being split apart. To study the "lists" of the spiritual gifts in Scripture see Romans 12:6-8; I Corinthians 12:8-10, 28-30; Ephesians 4:1-13; and I Peter 4:10, 11. It is a matter of opinion whether these lists were meant to be exhaustive, or whether they are simply examples. (For instance, what about musical talent, or other modern-day abilities that could be used in the church?)

Light on the Text

12:1-3   This is another topic the Corinthians had asked Paul about in their letter. Ignorance about spiritual gifts can have catastrophic effects—spectacular "spiritual" demonstrations can result in misplaced allegiance, similar to when the Corinthians were following dumb idols. Ignorance in spiritual gifts may result in terrible mistakes being made. Spiritually mature persons are to be judged by what they say, and only through the Holy Spirit could one be led to say that Jesus is Lord.

12:4-6 The word "gifts" is the Greek *charismata.* Arndt and Gingrich define the term as "special gifts of a non-material sort, bestowed by the grace of God on individual Christians."

Two other words are used in this passage to describe the special endowments enjoyed by Christians. Verse 5 mentions "service," from which our word "deacon" is derived. In verse 6, "working" is a translation of *energemata,* from which we get our word "energy." In each instance, Paul names a different member of the Godhead as a source of the gift ("the same Spirit," "the same Lord," "the same God"). Ray Stedman writes in *Body Life* (Regal Books) that "a gift is a specific capacity or function." Stedman says that "service" refers to the sphere where a gift is performed "among a certain group of people, or in a certain geographic area. It is the prerogative of the Lord Jesus to assign a sphere of service for each member of his body." "Working," or "energizings," refers to "the degree of power by which a gift is manifested or ministered on a specific occasion . . . . Every exercise of a spiritual gift does not produce the same result each time."

12:7-11 Spiritual gifts are given to every Christian for the good of the whole church. While the church is a unity, these gifts don't have to be uniform. All gifts proceed from God through the Spirit, and they are important enough for Him to determine what each member will receive. The unity of the body is exemplified by its response to suffering and honor. One part of the body does not suffer in isolation—pain involves the whole body. Likewise, when one part of the body is honored, the others participate in the accompanying rejoicing.

12:26-30 Each church member is a part of the Body of Christ, Paul says, applying the analogy he has formed. God himself took the active role of appointing people to certain gifts. The listing of gifts in verse 28 doesn't necessarily signify a consecutive ranking by importance, but it is noteworthy that tongues are listed last, since the Corinthians esteemed that gift so highly. A series of rhetorical questions shows that, in the experience of the church, a diversity of gifts exist and not every church member can perform a certain function.

12:31—
13:3
At the close of chapter 12, Paul says "And now I will show you the most excellent way." He reminds them no gift has value unless it is exercised in love.

Verse 1 refers to tongues, not because it is more important than the other gifts, but because of the undue emphasis the Corinthians placed on it. Pagan temples utilized large brass gongs as part of the worship ritual. Paul insists that unless persons speak in love, their gift is no better than the clanging heard in those temples.

"Prophecy" suggests the ability to speak for God. "Mysteries" are hidden things of God that can only be learned by divine revelation. "Knowledge" means wisdom gained through research and experience. Unless these are practiced in love, they will be of no value to his ministry. If the gift of faith is used to produce miracles but no caring love is exhibited, the faithful person is nothing to the strengthening of the Kingdom. Even generosity and martyrdom are profitless if they do not spring from love.

13:4-7
After establishing the preeminence of love, Paul turns to a portrayal of this active Christian concern. Take time to study in depth Paul's description of true, self-giving, Christian love. How would you rate the quality of your love relationships compared to the Biblical ideal?

13:8-13
However transient may be the other gifts of the Spirit, love never fails. It will continue into eternity. Prophecies and tongues, on the other hand, will be no more. Spirit-inspired knowledge will be discontinued, superseded by the immediate presence of reality.

In this life we understand life like a blurred image in a mirror. In ancient days a mirror was a piece of polished metal that gave an imperfect reflection. "Poor reflection" is the translation of a term from which our word "enigma" derives. "We see now through imperfect polished metal in an enigma," would be an accurate translation of the apostle's words. But in the day of Christ's appearing, we shall see "face to face."

14:1-5   "To prophesy" means to speak forth for God. This gift is superior to the gift of tongues, which edifies no one but the speaker unless the message is interpreted.

"Edifies" is the translation of a Greek word that means to build up others. Paul says in verse 3 that a prophet speaks "for their strengthening, encouragement and comfort." His proclamation must aim to build up the believers. It must aim to increase their knowledge of spiritual truth and enable them to live the Christian life.

The building up of the church is the purpose for which services are held; however, tongues cannot achieve this purpose unless an interpreter is present. But prophesying—speaking God's message in a clear manner—will always achieve the goal of edification.

14:6-11   Tongues have no value for edification unless an interpreter is present. If Paul came to Corinth and only spoke in tongues, he would be of less value to them. Words that don't communicate are meaningless, like a musical instrument that doesn't play an orderly tune or a trumpet that makes an imprecise tune instead of the one needed to call troops to battle.

The same is true in the church—unless we speak words that can be understood by all, we are misdirecting words into the air instead of at a particular person. There are a variety of languages in the world, yet they all have meaning, which is as God intended. If the meaning can't be transmitted, it is the same as though we are both foreigners. The Greek word for foreigners here is *barbaros*—from which we get "barbarian." Their incomprehensible tongues made the Corinthians little better than the uneducated barbarians to outsiders!

14:12-17   Paul urges the Corinthians to try to excel in the gifts that edify the church. Edification of the church through tongues only occurs if there is someone in the gathering who can interpret what is said. One who can speak in tongues should pray to receive the gift of being able to interpret the message as well. Otherwise, the person who prays in tongues is not using his or her understanding. Paul insists on the rightful place of the intellect in the exercise of all spiritual gifts.

In verses 16 and 17, Paul appears to be addressing the case of "inquirers," those who are interested in Christianity but had yet to make a commitment. Ecstatic prayer may have a detrimental effect on them. Again, Paul contrasts one worshiper's spiritual activities with the other person who doesn't "understand" (in his mind) and doesn't "know" (with his mind) what is being said. This spiritual growth process extends to the whole person, beyond mere spiritual or emotional excitement.

14:18-25 Paul turns to an argument in the Old Testament in Isaiah 28:9-12. The people of Israel did not listen to Isaiah when he preached to them in their own language, so he wrote of the time when the Assyrians would come and conquer them, after which they would have to listen to a language that they could not understand. Paul uses the argument to say tongues were meant for unbelieving people and were ineffective. While tongues are a sign for unbelievers, the gift can be misunderstood, and those that don't understand the gift may think the practitioners are insane! Prophecy, because it *can* be understood, can prompt conviction and repentance.

For Discussion

1. What is the relationship between natural talents and spiritual gifts?

2. What are the dominant principles a believer must consider in exercising spiritual gifts? If these concepts are so simple, why is it easy to lose sight of them?

3. What do others in your group say about your spiritual gifts? What are they? How do you use them?

Window on the Word

> This the secret of the holy,
> Not our holiness, but HIM:
> Jesus! empty us and fill us
> With Thy fulness to the brim.

8

The Reason for Our Confidence

Truth to Apply: Being confident of Christ's resurrection and return, I can endure whatever hardship confronts me in this life.

Key Verses: For what I received I passed on to you as of first importance: that Christ died for our sins according to the Scriptures, that he was buried, that he was raised on the third day according to the Scriptures, and that he appeared . . . (I Cor. 15:3-5a).

When you decide to fly in one of those 747 jumbo jets, it takes an incredible leap of faith. The plane itself weighs hundreds of thousands of pounds. Then, you pile on 300 passengers or so, all their luggage and an in-flight meal or two for each. Finally, for good measure, fill its gas tanks with 100,000 pounds of volatile jet fuel.

The part that requires faith is this—on the wings they put comparatively small jet engines. You're supposed to believe that they will propel the weighty plane into the sky merely by redistributing some air.

If you are a passenger, you can only hope the engineers that designed the plane didn't have faulty calculators! But have faith. You can go to an airport and watch 747 after 747 take off without a hitch.

It's not always that easy when it comes to some of our religious beliefs. We place our lives in the hands of God. We can't always see Him at work, and we certainly can't see into the future. The Corinthians questioned the resurrection of the dead, but Paul pointed to Christ's resurrection and said they could have faith in a God who has proved Himself faithful. How do you personally relate to an event that took place so long ago?

The Corinthians didn't deny Christ's resurrection, but some doubted the resurrection of others (see II Tim 2:18). Other cultures believed similarly. The Sadducees denied there was any Resurrection (Acts 23:6). The Greeks, who had an instinctive fear of death, believed in the immortality of the soul, but saw the body as an entrapment that would not be resurrected. For them, immortality could be achieved only by ridding themselves of their bodies. But for the Christian, the body is not evil, and the life to come will involve the whole human being, both body and soul. This is the position Paul pursues.

Light on the Text

15:1, 2   Paul begins by focusing on the basics of the Gospel, the Good News the Corinthians received from him and on the basis of which they achieve their stature in Christ. If their belief doesn't mirror the Gospel, they "have believed in vain"; they are not trusting totally in Christ, and their belief is groundless and empty.

15:3-7   The essence of the Gospel is that Christ died for our sins. Jesus act is consistent with predictions about the Messiah in the Old Testament, including His burial and resurrection on the third day. His rising from the dead was verified by Christ's appearance before Peter, James, the apostles, and to "more than 500 of the brothers at the same time." None of these appearances refer to specifically recorded accounts, but serve to show how well-based the evidence was for Christ's resurrection.

15:8-11   Finally, Christ appeared to Paul on the road to Damascus. He was "one abnormally born," not an apostle like the other 12, who had lived and walked with Christ. Rather, Christ appeared to him as one who did not even deserve to be an apostle because he had persecuted the early church. But he received God's unmerited favor, and that prompted him to work relentlessly, harder than others, who are unspecified. Yet even that could be attributed to God's grace.

15:12-19   The Gospel proclaims the fact of Christ's resurrection, so Paul asks how they could not believe in the resurrection of all believers. If there is no such resurrection, then Christ's rising could not have occurred. And Christ's resurrection plays so central a role in the theology of Christianity, that without it, their preaching and the Corinthians' resulting faith had no basis. If Christ's resurrection did not occur, the apostles would be false witnesses, saying God had done something that He had not. With no resurrection, faith is futile or vain, as other translations have it—with no content, no substance, nothing to distinguish it from other religions. Futile faith means the Corinthians are still mired in their sins.

Commenting on verse 17, Lutheran expositor R. C. H. Lenski observes, "To be in our sins equals [being] in their deadly sphere where all of our sins surround us and accuse us before God as so many deadly wolves about to tear us to pieces. Make the Savior what you please, if He failed to rise from the dead He is useless, for He cannot free us from our sins, the one thing for which we need a Savior. If there is no resurrection, there is also no redemption, no reconciliation with God, no justification, no life and salvation." If Christ hadn't risen, those believers who have died are without hope, and those who live hoping in Christ and looking to their own resurrection are deluding themselves.

15:20-28   Paul uses the figure of the firstfruits, derived from the Mosaic Law. It is the second significance of the Feast of the Passover, which also was a great harvest festival that occurred when the barley was due to be gathered. A sheaf of the firstfruits of the harvest was brought to the priest; it was ground in a barley mill and its flour was offered to God. This act had to be done before new barley could be bought and sold and made into bread. The firstfruits were a sign of the harvest to come, and so, too, was Christ.

Adam was originally responsible for humanity's "fall" into sin, which brought condemnation for each sinner. How appropriate for God to send another Man (fully human as Adam was, but also fully divine) to rectify the Adam in each of us and thus bring deliverance to all who trust Him. The promise of being set free from sin's curse is for those who are "in Christ." This means personally acknowledging Christ as Savior and Lord. Verses 25 and 26 remind us that Jesus came to earth as the Keystone in God's plan to defeat sin. "For this purpose the Son of God was manifested, that he might destroy the works of the devil" (I Jn. 3:8, KJV).

Father, Son, and Holy Spirit are a perfect unity. At the same time, each is an individual part of the Godhead. In verses 27 and 28, we glimpse some of the mystery of that relationship. Apparently Christ, the Son, has been delegated power by the Father to bring the present age to a close and inaugurate the fullness of God's Kingdom throughout the universe. This seems to mean that all things, except the Father Himself, will be subdued by the Son. Finally, the Son will voluntarily place Himself in subjection to the Father's full authority so that God, Three in One, shall be all in all.

15:29-34 The exact meaning of baptism for the dead is uncertain. Many theories exist, but one likely one is that Corinthian believers received baptized on behalf of others who had died before they were able to be baptized. While it's unlikely that Paul approved of the practice, he is able to use it in his argument. Such baptism would serve no purpose without the possibility of a resurrection. The peril in which believers live also must have a worthwhile reward, which is a life after death.

Paul uses himself as a prime example. It appears he was in some kind of danger in Ephesus (also noted in II Cor. 1:8-10) and, although unlikely he had to fight literal "wild beasts," he may be writing metaphorically of men who were seeking his death. If the dead are not raised, men and women might as well seek to maximize the enjoyment of this life. Such thinking is misleading and could corrupt the believers' good character.

15:35-38 Critics of the resurrection questioned the value of raising the decaying body out of the grave. Paul calls the argument foolish, giving as an example the sowing of seed, which dies to give birth to a new plant—more glorious than the former seed. Our current bodies aren't any indication of what our new bodies will be like. Divine oversight is mentioned in verse 38—God determines the plant that will grow out of each seed.

15:39-44 Similarly, not all earthly life is of the same "flesh." Paul's thought in verse 40 probably refers to the bodies of heavenly beings—having a different splendor than earthly bodies. He notes the differences between the splendor of sun, moon, and stars (vs. 41). This evidence can be extended to the improvement our resurrected bodies will be over the bodies laid in the grave. They will be raised spiritual bodies, fit for Heaven.

15:45-49 The order set forth in the idea of first Adam/last Adam implies the order—and something of the nature—of the transformation. Adam, the first of the human race, had his characteristics stamped upon it. Christ is the first of a race of new human beings. Adam came from dust; Christ's origination is heavenly. All are earthly, but Christians are also heavenly because of their relationship to Christ. At some point in the future, we will continually be like Him, bearing His likeness.

15:50-55 Because the resurrection of believers is assured and we will bear Christ's likeness, we can be sure that earthly bodies of flesh and blood won't be brought into the Kingdom. Our bodies all will be changed, although the exact extent of that change is a mystery. That change will occur in a flash (*atomos*—that which cannot be cut or divided). The twinkling of an eye means the time it takes to glance at something. The sound of the trumpet in Jewish tradition often is associated with the end times. At that time, the dead will be raised and all will be changed. The certainty is that resurrected bodies won't be affected by decay or threatened by death—though we don't know the exact nature of those bodies.

Knowing just this slight amount and that God is trustworthy, we become victors with Christ over death and sin. Paul quotes Isaiah 25:8 and then Hosea 13:14 to relate resurrection to the fulfillment of Scripture.

15:56-58 With death no longer a concern, the immediate threat is sin, which is overcome by the saving action of "our Lord Jesus Christ." It's by sin that death gained authority over humanity. Christ supercedes the power of sin and through Him we can move from certain defeat to certain victory. That should inspire believers to moral purity, not buffeted by circumstances or philosophies, and to earnest spiritual labor for the Lord.

For Discussion

1. What evidence do you see in this section for Christ's resurrection? If challenged by someone who did not believe, how would you support your belief in the bodily resurrection of Christ (or of life after death in general)?

2. Does Paul have an exact understanding of what will occur at the resurrection? What gives Paul confidence despite this lack of knowledge?

3. Most of us have a certain amount of fear regarding death. How do you experience that fear? How do you deal with it? In what ways does your theology help? What else helps?

Window on the Word

Life After Death?

For Christians, it is their experience and understanding of God which both makes life after death believable and suggests what form that life may take . . . . "If the individual can commune with God, then he must matter to God; and if he matters to God, he must share God's eternity. If God really rules, he cannot be conceived as scrapping what is precious in his sight."
(In Stephen H. Travis, *Christian Hope & The Future,* InterVarsity Press)

9

Handling Personal Conflicts

Truth to Apply: With Christ's comfort and strength, I can overcome personal conflicts and contribute to the restoration of fellowship in the church.

Key Verse: For just as the sufferings of Christ flow over into our lives, so also through Christ our comfort overflows (II Cor. 1:5).

A strong friendship can last forever. Unfortunately, we're just as likely to dislike someone for life. A lifetime of dislike separated Lady Astor and Winston Churchill. In one celebrated exchange, an exasperated Lady Astor told Churchill, "Winston, if I were married to you, I'd put poison in your coffee." Churchill quickly responded, "And if you were my wife, I'd drink it!"

Historians note that Abraham Lincoln was treated with contempt by Stanton, who was his war minister during the Civil War. Stanton called Lincoln "a low, cunning clown" and nicknamed him "the original gorilla." Lincoln, however, did nothing but treat him with courtesy. The kindness eventually won Stanton over. After Lincoln was assassinated, Stanton called Lincoln "the greatest ruler of men the world has ever seen." It's easy to acquire and keep hateful feelings toward people, even in the church. How can we exhibit a mature response to difficulties and conflicts?

The total number of letters Paul wrote from Ephesus to the church at Corinth is uncertain. We know Paul wrote I Corinthians from Ephesus. But in I Corinthians 5:9 Paul mentions a letter he had previously written. In it he had told the Corinthian Christians not to associate with "immoral men." This letter is lost. In II Corinthians, written from Macedonia, Paul refers to what is often called "the severe letter" (II Cor. 2:4; 7:8). Paul evidently had paid a brief visit to the Corinthians from Ephesus to try to correct their many problems, especially the rejection of his apostolic authority (II Cor. 2:1). Luke does not record this visit in Acts, perhaps because it was short and unsuccessful. The "severe letter" was written as a result of the "painful visit."

The sequence of events, then, was probably something like this: 1) Paul founds the Corinthian church (around A.D. 51); 2) Paul writes his first letter to Corinth (referred to in I Cor. 5:9); 3) Paul writes a second letter to Corinth, the letter we know as I Corinthians (written about A.D. 55); 4) Paul pays a painful visit to the Corinthians (referred to in II Cor. 2:1, 2); 5) Paul writes a third letter, severe in tone (referred to in II Cor. 2:4; 7:8); 6) Paul writes a fourth letter to Corinth, the letter we know as II Corinthians (written about A. D. 56); 7) Paul pays a third visit to Corinth (promised in II Cor. 12:14; 13:1, 2; probably included in Acts 20:2, 3).

Light on the Text

1:1, 2   Timothy, whose mission to Corinth is mentioned in I Cor. 16:10, joins Paul in greetings to the church at Corinth, which is God's own. The introduction shows that Paul expected the letter to be distributed to churches in the whole district of Achaia. At least two churches are known to have existed in this area (Athens, as indicated by Acts 17:34, and Cenchrea, mentioned in Rom. 16:1).

1:3-7   Paul begins his letter with a prayer of thanksgiving, praising God for the mercy and comfort he felt in situations he will describe in the following verses. He is the Father of compassion (other versions may read "mercies") and the God of all comfort. The Greek word for comfort, *paraclesis*, is similar to the word used for the Holy Spirit, *paracletos*, which means: "one called alongside [to help]." It occurs nine times in verses 3-7. The word can also mean encouragement and consolation. In difficult situations, God can encourage us to strive onward and be near us to provide intimate consolation. God's comfort allows us to be freed from concerns about our own difficulties. Paul associates his sufferings with those of Christ. He doesn't regret their enormity or frequency, seeing them as a way to obtain abundant blessing through Christ.

   Their sufferings and subsequent comforting will benefit the church at Corinth. Because Paul sees a purpose beyond the pain, it is endurable, and it enables him to experience the Lord's special intervention to comfort him. This serves as an example for Corinth, which the church also can apply.

1:8-11   The affliction that Paul suffered in Asia isn't specified and isn't recorded elsewhere. Some believe Paul was threatened by mob violence in Ephesus or serious illness. Whatever the specific problem, it appears Paul and his co-workers suffered greatly, "far beyond our ability to endure," so much so that they thought they wouldn't survive. But God delivered them from the danger, increasing their faith to believe that God will deliver them in the future. He alone is worthy of their hope.

1:12-14   Paul places his confidence in the fact that he had conducted his life with sincerity and holiness, both toward the Corinthian church and the world, not in the wisdom seen in those who are acting out of self-interest, but in actions that clearly show he is acting under and empowered by the grace of God. Paul's Letters to the

Corinthians exhibit the same characteristics. He expresses his gratefulness for the changes reported in their congregation, saying that he hopes they will be understanding of his actions and boast of him, just as Paul expects to boast of them when Christ returns to judge the world.

1:15-17 Paul's reason for asking for understanding is related to the many changes he made in his plans to visit Corinth. He had planned to visit the church on the way to and from Macedonia, but his decision to change plans wasn't a result of vacillation or the selfish considerations of those who would make plans "in a worldly manner." The Corinthians could hold such individuals in suspicion because they would vary their answers to their own best advantage. Paul wouldn't act in this way.

1:18-22 But flippant decisions aren't Paul's style. While the Corinthians may view Paul's actions in this way, it was not his intent. Jesus, preached among the believers at Corinth, did not act in this way, and Paul was following His example. All things promised about Christ in the Law and by the prophets had come true. Paul and the Corinthians have God in common, and in both their cases, He is making them firm and sure in their loyalty to Christ. God has consecrated them all to the service of Christ; He has set a seal upon them, a symbol of His ownership and their authentication; and He has acted to place the Spirit in their hearts as a down payment of the greater blessings that will come.

1:23—2:4 Paul defends his decision not to come to Corinth by saying he declined to come to spare them further sorrow. It was only in their best interests. Paul was not making these decisions as a despot who lorded his position over them; rather, they were co-workers in achieving spiritual growth, which would enable them to enjoy God's blessing. Paul would not make another painful visit to Corinth until he could be assured the situation there was improved. His purpose was not that he would grieve others so that he would be similarly grieved, but that their repentance would bring both them and him joy. He wrote the sorrowful letter not for the creation of sorrow, but as a way of expressing his love for them (Heb. 12:6, 10, 11; Rev. 3:19). Paul found the letter difficult to write—he wrote it out of great distress and anguish and with many tears, but in confidence that they would respond to his appeal.

2:5-11 The object of the sorrowful letter appears to be someone who had insulted Paul, either in his absence or during the apostle's last visit to the city. The pain he caused wasn't so much limited to Paul, but it was felt by the entire congregation. Paul says the punishment the offender received was sufficient; there is an implication that the offender is ready to repent. However, it appears there was a minority that either wanted the penalty to continue indefinitely or made harsher. Rather than continuing to drive him away from the fellowship of the church, Paul writes that they forgive and comfort him.

Verse 10 has been used in support of the common practice of more liturgical churches to pronounce the "affirmation of forgiveness." Such authority comes from Christ, mediated through the apostles.

Forgiveness is important so that the erring brother not experience excessive sorrow and thus become vulnerable to disillusionment and the power of Satan. This shows both the power of fellowship in influencing others' spirituality and, at the same time, the frailty of that walk and the nearness of Satan's power to a fellowship gone awry in purpose.

When an erring brother or sister has repented and turned from sin, the church must be quick to offer forgiveness and support. Yet, even if such a person never repents or changes, love and concern for his or her welfare must prevail among the other members. Fighting, resentment, and vindictiveness do terrible damage to the witness of any local church. They must be avoided at all costs. *Restoration of fellowship* is the prime motive of church discipline. Yet any kind of discipline—if used at all—must be used only as an absolute last resort. What better way to witness to God's love and accepting grace, than to treat one another with love?

For Discussion

1. What is bringing you the most pressure and despair at this moment? How has this seemed to surpass your own endurance? What experiences in your past help you to believe that God will supply strength and comfort in the future?

2. The Corinthians appear to have misunderstood Paul's change in traveling plans. What does Paul want them to do in verse 14? How can attempting to understand the other's situation limit difficulties in our fellowships?

3. Most people would agree that some kind of church discipline would help many of our churches today. Yet the whole concept can be grossly abused. Draw up a list of guidelines for dealing with continuous, evident sin in the lives of church members. Should anything be done—other than personal prayer for those involved? Discuss.

Window on the Word

Some commentators believe that II Corinthians is made up of fragments of letters. They see chapters 10 to 13 as possibly being a part of the sorrowful letter hinted at in II Cor. 2:4. The tone of this portion is not as complimentary as the previous chapters. Also, commentators see the section in 6:14 to 7:1 as possibly coming from the "previous letter" mentioned in I Cor. 5:9. This section seems to break a flow of thought and seems to bring in a set of ideas far different from the verses before or after. However, many of the explanations for this "creative editing" seem even more unlikely. R. V. G. Tasker writes "It would seem to be perfectly possible to trace sufficient unity of thought in the document as it stands at least to make it intelligible. The Epistle, as Menzies rightly says 'is all about a proposed visit.'. . . The apostle fears the false apostles at Corinth . . . who may make a further attempt to seduce the Corinthians from their loyalty."
(*II Corinthians,* InterVarsity Press)

10

The Call to Ministry

Truth to Apply: Having received the gift of salvation through Christ, I can now respond to His love by living a changed life before others.

Key Verse: We are therefore Christ's ambassadors (II Cor. 5:20a).

In a baseball game, performance often depends on a player's confidence. And perhaps no one had a better routine for destroying a batter's confidence than Ryne Duren, a relief pitcher during the 1950s and '60s. When he was called to pitch in a close ball game, he first would throw "warm-up" tosses. Invariably, his first warm-up toss would be extremely wild, often going way over the catcher's head. Duren, who wore thick glasses, would remove them, take a handkerchief from his pocket and slowly wipe them. After finishing his practice pitches, he would squint through his glasses in the general direction of the batter, whose confidence would now be quite shaky!

While we have the position of being Christ's ministers on earth, we often find it difficult to be brimming with confidence, especially when non-Christians throw a few wild shots about Christianity in our general direction. Rebecca Manly Pippert, an expert in evangelism, said she felt a "lack of faith and courage" in her first evangelistic efforts. But she realized that "when God is seeking a person, he will not allow my fear, my feeling of intimidation or my lack of knowledge or experience to prevent that person from finding him."

In your opinion, what is the best way to go about evangelizing a friend or neighbor? Where does the concept of ministry fit in?

Background/Overview: *II Cor. 2:12— 6:10*

In this section, Paul writes about various aspects of his ministry and how he approaches it. Here is an outline of this large portion of Scripture:

> The authentic minister, 2:12—3:5
> The minister's new message, 3:6-18
> The minister's mind-set, 4:1-18
> The minister's reward, 5:1-9
> The minister's compulsion, 5:10-19
> The minister's response, 5:20—6:10

Light on the Text

2:12, 13 Paul returns to describing his personal movements. He went to Troas to preach the Gospel when the Lord provided the opportunity, but he was so anxious for news from Titus that he left his work unfinished and went on to Macedonia to meet him and get his report.

2:14-16 The image Paul uses in verses 14-16 is that of a victorious Roman general leading a procession of soldiers, chariots, and prisoners through the streets of Rome. This procession, called a "triumph," was a mark of high honor and notable achievement for the conqueror.

The priests, marching with the procession, burned incense in thanksgiving to the heathen gods. To the crowds and soldiers, it was the odor of victory; to the prisoners chained to the chariot wheels, it was the odor of death and slavery. Paul sees himself as a part of this kind of procession, celebrating the victory of Christ in Corinth and affirming that God uses believers to manifest the life of Christ to others.

The word rendered "aroma" is regularly used of the Old Testament sacrifices. The meaning is evidently sacrificial. The image being communicated is that believers are the smoke or odor which rises from the sacrifice of Christ to God (see C. K. Barrett, *The Second Epistle to the Corinthians,* for more detail). This odor is a "*sweet* savour"—pleasing and acceptable to God.

Thus, Paul speaks of the life and message of believers (1) as a savor of life to those who accept the Gospel, and (2) as a savor of death to those who refuse the message of life.

2:17— 3:5   Paul neatly turns the accusation of his enemies against them by referring to a custom common at this time—the "epistles of commendation." Having spent 18 months in ministry in Corinth, Paul feels he does not need a letter of introduction (presumably the disrupters came with such letters); nor does he need a letter from the Corinthian church testifying to his effectiveness as a minister.

In a verse that is central to this study (vs. 2), Paul contrasts the written letter to the much superior "human letter." The Corinthians could not be ignorant of the authenticity of Paul's ministry. The Gospel had transformed their lives—a fact which bore testimony to "all men" that Paul's ministry was genuine.

3:6-11   The New Covenant (or "testament") of which Paul is a minister is based not on the letter of the law but on the Spirit. The Old Covenant was not a merely mechanical thing. It was a spiritual covenant. Its impact and position, however, were essentially external. It was too easy for the Jews to regard the Law as an instrument for human achievement.

The law contained glory, which Israel saw reflected in Moses' face (Ex. 34:29-35). But the new agreement with God contains even more glory because it is a ministry of righteousness in which those who believe are acquitted. By contrast, the Old Covenant, which lacked permanence, saw its glory fade, while the New Covenant's glory lasts forever.

3:12-18   The glory of the New Covenant of the Spirit prompts great boldness and a clear vision of the glory of God, knowing that the glory will not be superseded, as was the case with Moses. That prophet veiled his face because he knew the glory was fading, Paul contends. But the Israelites didn't understand that this meant that the Old Covenant would fade also.

The Spirit of the Lord offers this liberty in order to remove one from under the Law, and to illuminate sin and its inevitable penalty. No longer under compulsion, we are free to serve God freely, of our own accord.

4:1-12 Paul doesn't lose heart in the face of accusations. Those filed against him apparently include that he used underhanded methods, cleverness to get his own way and that he changed the Word of God. Continuing to proclaim the Gospel was his only defense.

Those who don't understand the Gospel are perishing because they choose not to believe, blinded by the "god of this age" (the Devil). When this god is present, an individual is shrouded in a darkness that even the Gospel cannot penetrate.

The call to share the Gospel is a treasure, and it has been entrusted to those who have limitations and shortcomings—in this way, others can see it truly is power from God. Not only are ministers of humble, unspectacular origins, but they are subject to, and not protected from, a variety of pressures not necessarily common to others (vss. 8, 9). Their lives reflect the sacrificial nature exhibited by Jesus, and they feel like they are under the sentence of death. Though "death is at work in us" in that way, their lives portray the story of Christ and His gift of life to all.

4:13-15 Quoting Psalm 116:10, Paul writes that speaking is a natural response to belief. He speaks in spite of dangers, knowing that an eventual victory and reward are promised—God will raise Paul, and his joy will be multiplied because his Corinthian converts will be there as well. His efforts are for their benefit, his purpose that more will believe and join in praise to God.

4:16-18 As a result of the promises accruing to Paul and his fellow ministers, they do not lose heart. While the physical body wastes away, there is inward renewal and the things of the Spirit assume more importance.

The glorious eternal reward reserved for God's

servants, while not seen, is so great that current affliction is comparatively light and momentary.

5:1-10   Here Paul goes into detail about the difference between the existence in Heaven and our earthly existence. How would you respond to someone who says this is all just "pie in the sky"?

5:11-17   Paul's theme in verse 14 is not his own love of Christ, but Christ's love for him.

Two profound truths are expressed in the succinct statement "one died for all, and therefore all died." The first is the substitutionary aspect of the atonement.

The second truth is our participation in this death. Some interpreters believe "Christ's death was the death of all, in the sense that He died the death they should have died" (Tasker). Many other commentators think this is not the death from which we have been rescued, but the mystical joining with Christ in His death.

In the New Testament, the death of Christ constantly is associated with His resurrection. Death without resurrection is defeat.

By human standards, Christ was a failure. The few followers He attracted fled when times became difficult, and He died an ignominious death by execution. He gained no kingdom and no fortune. Paul himself later tried to exterminate His followers. But Christ no longer was viewed that way by Paul. Similarly, no longer are believers to be evaluated "from a worldly point of view"—more specifically, by human standards—for they are all transformed into changed creations in which the old is disappearing.

5:18-21   In verse 18 we see that it is God who reconciles us to Himself. Paul mentions the apostolic commission to carry this message to the world. The message we bring is that we can be righteous—considered innocent—before God through Christ, who through the plan of God, took our sin on Himself and paid the penalty of death.

Christ was and remains always the sinless One. Verse 21 does not say that God made Him a *sinner*. But He received the awful judgment of sin—our sin—for us. And for those in Christ the result is their standing before God in righteousness.

6:1-10   In II Corinthians 6, Paul exhorts the Corinthians to live up to the Gospel which has been entrusted to them. We are, he says first of all, "fellow workers" with God.

What does it mean to receive the Gospel "in vain"? The word comes from a root meaning "empty." The content of the Gospel we preach must be matched by the way it fills our lives.

Paul, while reluctant to commend himself, here does so to show the credit of his ministry. He ends this section by using a series of contrasts to compare others' views of him and God's view of him.

For Discussion

1. What responses should the New Covenant provoke in us? What difference would it make in your life if you were more conscious of "reflecting the Lord's glory"?

2. How can chapter 4 better enable us to endure hardships?

3. Our bodies are wasting away, yet we can look forward to an eternal abode in Heaven. How does this make you feel?

4. How are you now responding to God's call to personal ministry? In what ways would you like to become more effective?

Window on the Word

Keeping the Aquarium

With all our education, our fine buildings, our image of the church, we are doing less to win people to Christ than our unschooled forefathers did. We're no longer fishers of men, but keepers of the aquarium, and we spend most of our time swiping fish from each other's bowl.

(Dr. Kermit Long, *Christian Victory*)

11

A Cause for Joy

Truth to Apply: My love for fellow believers motivates me to help them shun sin and pursue God.

Key Verse: Yet now I am happy, not because you were made sorry, but because your sorrow led you to repentance. For you became sorrowful as God intended and so were not harmed in any way by us (II Cor. 7:9).

Those who teach and instruct others often have a profound impact on the lives of their students. The effect they have often goes far beyond the knowledge they transmit, and the way they handle difficulties with students and correct them often has a lifelong impact.

One high school student taking a class in woodshop was a bit hesitant to work with power tools. In one class the instructor showed her how to use a router to make a design on the edge of a wood project. One of the instructor's warnings was not to press too hard or the cutting blade would burn the wood.

The student began to work. For 20 minutes, she gingerly used the router and pressed lightly so as not to burn the wood. However, the intermittent whine of the machine in the hands of the inexperienced student aggravated the teacher to such a point that he stormed over, grunted "Give me that!" and grabbed the router out of her hands—finishing the project in a few seconds. The heavy pressure he used left deep burn marks in the wood. While several hours of sanding replaced that damage, the student never could erase the humiliation. She never again considered working with wood.

Correcting and directing others is always difficult, but especially so in the church. How should we approach it? What guidelines should we use?

II Corinthians is a letter written by an author experiencing emotional peaks and valleys. He loved the Corinthian church dearly, but had to send a harsh and pointed letter to them through Titus. Later, Titus's positive report meant the relationship had been restored, to Paul's great joy.

Intimately sharing his sufferings and commitment to the ministry, Paul no doubt felt especially close to the Corinthians, and that love asks for the same kind of love in return. It is out of his love and desire for intimate unity that he orders they not be intimately involved with nonbelievers, and 6:14—7:1 is a parenthetical statement related to his main thrust.

This portion contains a glimpse at the trauma involved in discipline and the joy resulting from effective and true repentance.

Light on the Text

6:11-13 Paul has shared the intimate details of his life and ministry with the Corinthians, exposing his deepest emotions about them. By directly addressing them, he shows his deep feelings. In his other letters, Paul rarely addresses the group by name (Gal. 3:1 and Phil. 4:15 are the only instances). Paul sees their response of affection as limited. He cares for them as he would care for his own children, and he asks that they reciprocate with a "fair exchange"—that they return in an equivalent amount—the affection he has exhibited.

6:14-16a Paul interupts his plea for closer fellowship by directing that the Corinthians sever close relations with nonbelievers. Already in his letters to this church, Paul has noted that Christians cannot isolate themselves from the world (I Cor. 5:9). Existing "mixed" marriages were to be maintained and, in some instances, it was permissible to dine with idol-worshipping neighbors (I Cor. 7:12; 10:17). However, close partnership involves being of the same mind, especially in the spiritual dimension, and breeds loyalty. Christians are not to be bound to unbelievers in areas such as marriage and ecclesiastical relations. Paul's illustrations are from the Old Testament, referring to Deut. 22:10 "Do not plow with an ox and a donkey yoked together." The Corinthians are not to be stained by lawlessness or have their holiness spoiled by sin. Paul uses a series of three rhetorical questions, culminating with the impossibility of fellowship between Christ and Satan, to develop the answer for a fourth rhetorical question, which shows that believers have virtually nothing of eternal value in common with nonbelievers. The fifth rhetorical question continues the impossibility of agreement between the temple of God—His Church, which has been set apart for His purpose—and idols.

6:16b-18 The Old Testament supports the idea that, as God's people, we have an intimate relationship with Him that requires us to be holy, clean, and dealing with personal evil. In return, God promises fellowship with us, acceptance of us and a close familial relationship. In addition to the quotation from Leviticus, Paul quotes from Isaiah 52:11; Ezekiel 20:34; and II Samuel 7:14. It is interesting to note that none of these verses are quoted verbatim, primarily because Paul is quoting them from memory. Locating the exact verse on papyrus scrolls would have been a slow, painstaking task. Paul shows no reluctance to quote the verses as long as the substance of the verses is correct.

7:1 In light of the promises of God's presence and fellowship with us, we should aim to practice and grow in holiness, separating ourselves from those things that would act to defile us. We should strive for holiness because reverence before God is the attitude that controls our lives.

7:2-4 Paul renews his plea of 6:13. He deserves to be accepted because they have no reason to be restrained in their feelings toward him. The charges leveled against him were false. He doesn't mount this defense as a way of condemning the Corinthians for what his critics have said. He is loyal to them, having great confidence in them, taking pride in their growth to date and encouraged that they will continue to mature. Despite all the difficulties he personally has endured, Paul is jubilant.

7:5-7   This is related to what Paul was discussing in 2:13, where Paul first mentioned that he could not continue his work in Troas without knowing the outcome of the Corinthian situation. He left for Macedonia to meet Titus so he could get the information as soon as possible. The period of waiting was difficult. Paul had to endure external harassment and internal worry over the response to the severe letter. He was downcast during this period of waiting, but that turned to joy when Titus told of his reception in Corinth, their repentance and their actions that comforted Titus. Far from a negative reaction to the severe letter, the Corinthians responded by reaffirming their affection, feeling sorrow for their shortcomings and the injury to Paul and exhibiting concern for him. This dramatic turn of events evoked great joy in the apostle.

7:8-12   Paul agonized over the severe letter as he wrote it (2:4) and, for a short while, had second thoughts about sending it. But even though it had caused them pain and sorrow, they had repented as a result of it. For that, Paul was happy and no longer regretted the letter. The word repentance carries with it the idea of seeking God's forgiveness and submitting one's conduct to God's standard—in short, turning from sin to God. This is one of the chief accomplishments of godly sorrow, one of the evidences that the Holy Spirit is working in a person (Jn. 16:8, 9), and one designed by God. Unlike worldly sorrow, godly sorrow does not cause the believer to regret experiencing it—rather, it causes the believer to turn from sin, accept and appreciate his or her salvation from God, and this causes peace and happiness. The world's sorrow is often only remorse that something has occurred and that one has experienced pain. In those cases it does not result in repentance or salvation, thus leading to death—there is no positive effect. But the repentance brought about by godly sorrow is typified by the traits in verse 11. We can assume that worldly sorrow is characterized by lesser degrees or the antitheses of these traits. However, the most important result of the severe letter was not the punishment of the one who had wronged Paul, but rather to show the Corinthians how highly they regarded Paul.

7:13-16 Paul was encouraged not only by the Corinthians' affirmation of him, but also by the heartwarming reception that they had shown to Titus (perhaps in contrast with the way they had dealt with Timothy in his visit mentioned in I Cor. 16:10, 11). Titus had returned refreshed, and Paul was relieved that those at Corinth had lived up to the praise. Their obedience and anxiousness to please increased Titus's affection and admiration—there is much to be admired about an individual or church that responds to discipline as the Corinthian church did. Paul's confidence in their spiritual direction is now complete.

For Discussion

1. Why do you think it is important for a church to have a "fair exchange of openness and intimacy"? What could you do to improve this "exchange" at your church?

2. Give an example of a way you have had to change a relationship or a life-style to avoid being "unequally yoked." What are the consequences of such relationships?

3. Review the characteristics of godly sorrow. What can you do to make the sorrow you experience more godly and less worldly?

4. What do we learn about the godly response to discipline? Are you as willing to be disciplined as you are to discipline? Share.

Window on the Word

If you commit yourself to Jesus Christ, you automatically

change every other relationship in your life. When he becomes supreme to you, other people slip into different places. Those nearest you may become alienated. Those who you once abhorred will become dear and intimate. The question of future marriage assumes a new solemnity. The re-evaluation and reorientation that follow commitment apply not only to values, but also to people. For example, "to hate one's family" (Mt. 10:32-39) means to be so committed to Christ that however much it costs to be away from that circle, I must cut myself ruthlessly from its comfort and follow him . . . .

(*The Cost of Commitment*, John White)

12

The Fellowship of Giving

Truth to Apply: When I am generous in my giving, I bring honor to God and blessing to others.

Key Verse: There is no need for me to write to you about this service to the saints (II Cor. 9:1).

No one is more synonymous with wealth than Howard Hughes. He accumulated billions of dollars through an industrial empire that employed hundreds of thousands of workers. Yet Hughes will be remembered as a sad, pitiful figure, especially in his final years. He was a recluse whom no one saw, who lived in terror, who had only a few friends and who died alone. History will remember his flamboyant activities in the 1930s and '40s, but its lesson will be that great wealth drove a man to a miserable existence. In 25 years, few will remember Howard Hughes, or want to remember him.

One who will be remembered forever, however, is someone who is at the other extreme from Howard Hughes. This woman, a widow, had a bank account that showed only two coins of copper, the smallest amounts of coinage in use in her day. One day, she took the two coins, went to the Temple, and gave them to the treasury. Two coins—total value of about two cents. Her life savings—one can almost imagine the coffer laughing at the small gift. But it caught the attention of one man, and the Lord Jesus used her example as a graphic picture of what it means to give to God one's all (Mk. 12:41-44). Paul also addresses our willingness and motivations for giving in this chapter. In what way and with which attitude should we approach this area? How can we become "better givers"?

Now on his third missionary journey, Paul was promoting a special campaign to raise money for the needy Christians in Jerusalem.

The *Expositor's Bible Commentary* offers five reasons why the Christians in Jerusalem were poor: "(1) After their conversion to Christianity many Jews in Jerusalem would have been ostracized socially and economically. (2) The experiment in community sharing described in Acts 2:44, 45, and 4:32, 34, 35 undoubtedly would have aggravated, though it did not cause, their poverty. (3) Persistent food shortages in Palestine because of overpopulation culminated in the famine of A.D. 46 in the time of Emperor Claudius (Acts 11:27-30). (4) As the mother-church of Christendom, the Jerusalem church was obliged to support a proportionately large number of teachers and probably to provide hospitality for frequent Christian visitors to the holy city. (5) Jews in Palestine were subject to a crippling two-fold taxation— Jewish and Roman." Besides his obvious aim of helping the destitute, Paul also wanted to create a tangible expression of Christian unity. For if Christ had really brought a new race of people into being who were neither Jew nor Gentile (Eph. 2:13-18), here was an opportunity to show this was true.

Light on the Text

8:1-6 While the main burden of Paul's second Letter to the Corinthians is his defense of his ministry and apostleship, chapters 8 and 9 are an interlude in which he appeals to the Corinthians to complete the collection that they had started for the Jerusalem poor. His appeal begins with a report of the liberality of the Macedonian churches (Thessalonica, Philippi, Berea) which were undergoing persecution and whose financial resources were very limited (8:1, 2). In spite of their own predicament, they gave above their ability (8:3), begging to be allowed to participate in the fund-raising drive. Paul calls this willingness the grace of God (8:1). The Macedonians gave with overflowing joy and rich generosity, which is a result of being conscious of the great generosity exhibited by God in giving His Son to reconcile us to Himself. Our giving should be without stipulation, as God's was without stipulation. Paul goes on to characterize the Macedonians' giving by saying it went beyond money, even though they had given miraculously, far beyond what they could afford. They gave themselves to the Lord first and then to the apostles for the service of Christ. Often enough, it's easy to give monetarily as a substitute for surrender to God or sacrificial service in a church. But this attitude among the Macedonians makes it easy to understand how they could plead for opportunities to share in the collection and give so abundantly. Their generosity prompted Paul to help the Corinthians complete their own collection.

8:7-9 The Corinthians already had showed they were dedicated to the practice and development of their other spiritual gifts. Paul urged them (because he did not want to command them) to seek to cultivate the gift of giving, which serves to show the sincerity of their love. We can be encouraged to give by the example of Christ, who sacrificed his position and wealth as God to become a man so that He might die and take all the sins of mankind upon Himself. He did this so we could share His heavenly wealth.

8:10-12 Paul states his words as advice, not a command. A year ago, the Corinthians had exhibited their eagerness to help in this collection, and that had stimulated the Macedonians to give so impressively. Now, it was time for them to complete the action they began a year ago and finish their collection. The amount to be donated is not a named percentage or amount, but should be determined by the extent of their means. What supersedes the amount is the willingness with which it is given.

8:13-15 Another principle determining the amount of the gift is that of equality. Paul didn't intend that the Corinthians give so much that they would be in poverty and the recipients would be living in ease. The ideal would be that the Corinthians would be giving out of their abundance so those in need could have enough to have what they needed to survive. Someday, the roles might be reversed, and then, the principle of equality would save the Corinthians. The principle of equality is seen in Exodus 16:18, as God supplied manna in the wilderness, enabling the Israelites to survive.

8:16-24 Paul's plan for bringing the collection to Jerusalem is devised in such a way that no one could accuse him of any impropriety. Titus accepted the task of helping the Corinthians gather their collection. He and two other believers (the one mentioned in verse 18 traditionally has been identified as Luke, although there is no evidence to substantiate it) would accompany the gift as Paul brought it to Jerusalem. "All the churches" selected the first brother for this mission, and the second is commended by his zeal and his confidence in the Corinthians. These intricate plans are intended to ensure that the impact of the gift isn't lessened by suspicion of Paul. Rather, the gift is meant to honor the Lord and show to fellow believers the Corinthians' eagerness to help. This will occur only if their actions are proper in the sight of the Lord, and of the world. The Corinthians are to show proof of their love by completing the collection.

9:1-5 The Corinthians knew the details of the needs of the Jerusalem church. When the idea was introduced, they were so eager to help that Paul had boasted about their readiness to the Macedonians, and that prodded them to give. Paul is sending Titus and the two brothers so that the collection can continue and so the boasts Paul made about the Corinthians would be true. It would be particularly embarrassing if some of the Macedonians might come to Corinth and their collection was incomplete. A gift "grudgingly given" does not benefit the giver. Instead, the act of giving is seen as a distasteful obligation if the gift is obtained through pressure.

For Discussion

1. What is the basic contrast between the churches at Macedonia and Corinth? Why is talk so cheap and action so difficult? Give an example from your own spiritual journey.

2. What positive lessons on giving can we learn from the Macedonian church? Which one do you most need to emulate? How do you intend to do so this week?

3. How can the concept of equality apply to us today? Can your church or fellowship logically be expected to adhere to the principle in this day and age? How?

4. What promises does God give concerning the giver? What difference would it make in your life if you could have complete faith in these promises? What holds us back from such complete faith?

Window on the Word

I already have confessed that I don't know what the treasure [in heaven] is [Mt. 6:20]. Obviously, it is valuable to us hereafter. Just as obviously, it will not cause us the anxiety earthly investments do. Securities belie their name. Banks and insurance companies will pass away. Precious metals have all through history been stolen. There is no such thing on earth as a safe investment—not even a fairly safe one. But heavenly treasure is guaranteed by the Name of Jehovah. It is of value. It is secure . . . It is interesting to notice how different treasures affect people. Pearls, diamonds and gold are associated with piracy, theft, murder, holdups, anxiety, greed, cruelty, torture. The longing to possess them awakens unwholesome passions in men. What if the "treasure" were an increased capacity to appreciate Christ (as many commentators suggest)? Certainly a longing to know Christ in all his beauty has very different effects on Christians than the chance of making a million dollars.

(*The Cost of Commitment*, John White)

13

Pretenders to Paul's Crown

Truth to Apply: When facing church leadership conflict situations, I must look beyond the surface to see the underlying motives and in whom God's power is revealed.

Key Verses: Now I am ready to visit you for the third time, and I will not be a burden to you, because what I want is not your possessions but you. So I will very gladly spend for you everything I have and expend myself as well. If I love you more, will you love me less? (II Cor. 12:14a, 15).

Almost every company has an organizational chart, which consists of several boxes and lines that connect them. Its purpose is simple—a chart is used to show who is responsible for a company's products and services and to establish who reports to whom in the company.

Despite the best plans, an organization can be so complex that two people may have authority over several employees or even over an entire division. In cases like this, production can suffer and bickering and power plays increase. The company must move quickly to resolve situations where leadership is in question.

Similar confusion was occurring at Corinth, as the authority of the church was in doubt. What criteria did the church there need to decide intelligently? What were Paul's qualifications?

Background/Overview: *II Cor. 10:1—13:14*

In II Corinthians, Paul has dealt with or alluded to attacks being made on him (II Cor. 1:17; 3:1), and now he confronts the situation head-on in a lengthy defense of himself and his ministry. He notes that when he visits Corinth the third time, the situation will come to a head if it is not resolved beforehand (II Cor. 13:1-3).

In this section, Paul turns his attention to a minority who have turned their loyalty to false leaders who lifted up their own position by making a series of charges against Paul, hoping to discredit him. These "super-apostles" (11:5) apparently sought to have the new Gentile converts submit to some of the Jewish customs.

Light on the Text

10:1-6   Paul is writing to some who have switched loyalty from him to the false shepherds, changing his writing style from using a plural pronoun to a first person pronoun. Evidently, the false apostles contended that Paul was timid in person compared with the powerful nature of his letters (verse 1). They also contended that Paul lived by the "standards of this world," the impulses of the sinful nature. Paul counters these arguments by saying he will be bold when he next returns. He notes that the weapons he uses in spiritual warfare would not succeed if they were only of the world. The nature of his accomplishments show they are backed by divine power.

10:7-11   The Corinthians are accepting these false apostles without looking at their motives. They exhibit confidence in themselves and disdain for Paul, but they must realize Paul belonged to Christ as much as they do. Paul has more authority because of the supernatural calling he experienced, and he used his apostleship to build up the church, not tear it down.

Paul's letters, although powerful and deep in

theological thought, were not meant to merely frighten the Corinthians. Nor was his appearance and speaking abilities meant to be ridiculed and lessen the importance of what he was saying. While Paul preferred to act in a meek and gentle way, he would come and act forcefully if necessary.

10:12-18 Paul did not want to put himself in the class with or compare himself with those who only have self-commendation for credentials. It is easy to have a lofty concept of oneself if one's measuring stick and basis for comparison is oneself, but such a practice is unwise (vs. 12), invites exaggeration (vs. 15) and ignores God's assessment. Paul would not appropriate unearned honor for himself, accepting it only in the areas where God allowed him to minister. Paul was prepared to enter other mission fields, but the problem of the false apostles at Corinth was delaying him. As the Corinthian church became more self-sufficient, Paul could expand to preach in other areas.

11:1-6 Paul uses a picture from Jewish marriage customs, specifically that of having "friends" of the bridegroom. They performed many duties, but chief among them was to ensure the chastity of the bride. In the marriage of the Corinthian church and Jesus Christ, Paul sees himself as a friend of the bridegroom.

Following Christ in devotion involves simplicity and holiness, but some would deflect the Corinthians from that aim, using deception and craftiness. They were seeking to improve the Gospel, and thus wound up preaching a different Christ and a different Gospel. The Corinthians willingly accepted the message of those false apostles. Paul merits the same kind of attention, even though he is not eloquent, because of the knowledge of God he possesses.

11:7-12 Paul's critics apparently said he didn't accept support because his teaching wasn't worth anything, and this invalidated his work. But Paul said his real motive was that the Corinthians might be elevated—in this way, they could focus their attention on the content of the message and not the amount of money it was costing them to hear it. While Paul was at Corinth, he was supported by other churches, notably the Macedonian church, so that he would not be under obligation to the Corinthians. Paul appears to be consistent in this philosophy, and he follows it so that he would be unencumbered by obligations and so there would be no charges that he was ministering only for financial gain. His reasons are not motivated by pride, but by love for the Corinthians.

11:13-15	Those who called themselves "super-apostles" are, in fact, false, deceitful and merely masquerading, just as Satan does when he poses as an angel of light. The false apostles put on a disguise that allows them to trick others into believing they are righteous, but God, who sees the heart, will give them what their destructive actions deserve.
11:16-21	Paul is no fool, but since the Corinthians are willing to hear the boasts of worldly men, they should give a hearing to his credentials. By contrast, the false apostles commended themselves and showed the Corinthians anything but love. Where Paul aimed to elevate them (v. 7), the false apostles enslaved them, perhaps to following Jewish laws. The false apostles exploit and take advantage of the Corinthians. Paul sarcastically says he was too "timid" to try anything like that!
11:22-29	The false apostles apparently boasted that they spoke ancient Hebrew and were Abraham's descendants. What they boasted of, Paul also could claim. He doesn't dispute their first three qualifications, but seems to question whether they indeed are serving Christ. In any case, he has been a harder working servant. His sacrifices for the Kingdom are listed in verses 23-28. They can be grouped into sacrifices of punishment, travel hardships and hardships of life. In addition, he is weighed down by the fatherly concern he has for the churches he has started.
11:30-33	Paul's list of commendations really detail his humiliations and sufferings. As such, he would rather boast of his weaknesses, because in spite of them, the Lord has used Paul. He recounts his escape from Damascus, perhaps as

an embarrassment because he fled from his pursuers and may not have trusted God for protection.

12:1-6 Paul's opponents might have been citing visions as one of their points of commendation. Paul recounts an ecstatic supernatural experience in which he was near God in a mystical moment that Christ enabled him to see. He refers to it as another man's experience, but writes that he was brought up to the third heaven or paradise. Paradise comes from a Persian word that originally referred to the walled garden of a Persian king. A king who wanted to give a citizen a special honor would allow that person to be a "companion of the garden," permitting him to walk in the garden and have an intimate relationship with the king. Paul would boast of such indications of God's special blessing upon him, but while he has much to boast of and it is all true, he refrains from doing so because it can be misinterpreted.

12:7-10 Almost every commentator has a theory on Paul's thorn in the flesh—theories range from persecution to his physical appearance, bouts with epilepsy, severe headaches, malarial fever and eye trouble. Whatever the outward form, it was Satan's messenger. Paul's repeated prayers did not remove the thorn, but he instead learned a more valuable lesson. He could draw upon God's power, and it would be sufficient. Moreover, the weakness would better reveal God's power, thus enhancing Paul's efforts.

For Discussion

1. What qualities should a minister of the Gospel possess?

2. How grave is the problem presented by the false apostles? How does Paul attack this problem? What is his prime motivation?

3. What would you consider your "thorn in the flesh"? In what ways can you emulate Paul's attitude to cope with this thorn?

Window on the Word

Some Bible scholars believe the severe letter, or parts of it, is actually II Corinthians 10—13. They believe it was somehow joined with the other, later epistle to Corinth. They chiefly hold this view because in II Corinthians 10—13, Paul uses strong language against those who oppose him after he has spent much of his time up to that point commending the Corinthians for their change of heart. In the absence of any manuscript support for this hypothesis, however, it is reasonable to assume that no mixing up of Paul's letters took place. Indeed, the tone of II Corinthians 10—13 is not as harsh as Paul's words about the severe letter would lead us to believe they would be. The change in tone from commendation to condemnation can be understood as Paul's warning to any lingering opposition.

Leader Helps and Lesson Plan

General Guidelines for Group Study

*Open and close each session with prayer.

*Since the lesson texts are not printed in the book, group members should have their Bibles with them for each study session.

*As the leader, prepare yourself for each session through personal study (during the week) of the Bible text and lesson. On notepaper, jot down any points of interest or concern as you study. Jot down your thoughts about how God is speaking to you through the text, and how He might want to speak to the entire group. Look up cross-reference passages (as they are referred to in the lessons), and try to find answers to questions that come to your mind. Also, recall stories from your own life experience that could be shared with the group to illustrate points in the lesson.

*Try to get participation from everyone. Get to know the more quiet members through informal conversation before and after the sessions. Then, during the study, watch for nonverbal signs (a change in expression or posture) that they would like to respond. Call on them. Say: "What are your thoughts on this, Sue?"

*Don't be afraid of silence. Adults need their own space. Often a long period of silence after a question means the group has been challenged to do some real thinking—hard work that can't be rushed!

*Acknowledge each contribution. No question is a dumb question. Every comment, no matter how "wrong," comes from a worthy person, who needs to be affirmed as valuable to the group. Find ways of tactfully accepting the speaker while guiding the discussion back on track: "Thank you for that comment, John; now what do some of the others think?" or, "I see your point, but are you aware of . . . ?"

When redirecting the discussion, however, be sensitive to the fact that sometimes the topic of the moment *should be* the "sidetrack" because it hits a felt need of the participants.

*Encourage *well-rounded* Christian growth. Christians are called to grow in knowledge of the Word, but they are also challenged to grow in love and wisdom. This means that they must constantly develop in their ability to wisely apply the Bible knowledge to their experience.

Lesson Plan

The following four-step lesson plan can be used effectively for each chapter, varying the different suggested approaches from lesson to lesson.

STEP 1: *Focus on Life Need*

The opening section of each lesson is an anecdote, quote, or other device designed to stimulate sharing on how the topic relates to practical daily living. There are many ways to do this. For example, you might list on the chalkboard the group's answers to: "How have you found this theme relevant to your daily life?" "What are your past successes, or failures, in this area?" "What is your present level of struggle or victory with this?" "Share a story from your own experience relating to this topic."

Sharing questions are designed to be open-ended and allow people to talk about themselves. The questions allow for sharing about past experiences, feelings, hopes and dreams, fears and anxieties, faith, daily life, likes and dislikes, sorrows and joys. Self-disclosure results in group members' coming to know each other at a more intimate level. This kind of personal sharing is necessary to experience deep affirmation and love.

However you do it, the point is to get group members to share *where they are now* in relation to the Biblical topic. As you seek to get the group involved, remember the following characteristics of good sharing questions:[1]

1. Good sharing questions encourage risk without forcing participants to go beyond their willingness to respond.

90

2. Good sharing questions begin with low risk and build toward higher risk. (It is often good, for instance, to ask a history question to start, then build to present situations in people's lives.)

3. Sharing questions should not require people to confess their sins or to share only negative things about themselves.

4. Questions should be able to be answered by every member of the group.

5. The questions should help the group members to know one another better and learn to love and understand each other more.

6. The questions should allow for enough diversity in response so each member does not wind up saying the same thing.

7. They should ask for sharing of self, not for sharing of opinions.

STEP 2: *Focus on Bible Learning*

Use the "Light on the Text" section for this part of the lesson plan. Again, there are a number of ways to get group members involved, but the emphasis here is more on learning Bible content than on applying it. Below are some suggestions on how to proceed. The methods could be varied from week to week.

*Lecture on important points in the Bible passage (from your personal study notes).

*Assign specific verses in the Bible passage to individuals. Allow five or ten minutes for them to jot down 1) questions, 2) comments, 3) points of concern raised by the text. Then have them share in turn what they have written down.

*Pick important or controversial verses from the passage. In advance, do a personal study to find differences of interpretation among commentators. List and explain these "options" on a blackboard and invite comments concerning the relative merits of each view. Summarize and explain your own view, and challenge other group members to further study.

*Have class members do their own outline of the Bible passage. This is done by giving an original title to each section, chapter, and paragraph, placing each under its appropriate heading according to subject matter. Share the outlines and discuss.

*Make up your own sermons from the Bible passage. Each sermon could include: Title, Theme Sentence, Outline, Illustration, Application, Benediction. Share and discuss.

*View works of art based on the text. Discuss.

*Individually, or as a group, paraphrase the Bible passage in your own words. Share and discuss.

*Have a period of silent meditation upon the Bible passage. Later, share insights.

STEP 3: *Focus on Bible Application*

Most adults prefer group discussion above any other learning method. Use the "For Discussion" section for each lesson to guide a good discussion on the lesson topic and how it relates to felt needs.

Students can benefit from discussion in a number of important ways:[2]

1. Discussion stimulates interest and thinking, and helps students develop the skills of observation, analysis, and hope.

2. Discussion helps students clarify and review what they have learned.

3. Discussion allows students to hear opinions that are more mature and perhaps more Christlike than their own.

4. Discussion stimulates creativity and aids students in applying what they have learned.

5. When students verbalize what they believe and are forced to explain or defend what they say, their convictions are strengthened and their ability to share what they believe with others is increased.

There are many different ways to structure a discussion. All have group interaction as their goal. All provide an opportunity to share in the learning process.

But using different structures can add surprise to a discussion. It can mix people in unique ways. It can allow new people to talk.

Total Class Discussion

In some small classes, all students are able to participate in one effective discussion. This can build a sense of class unity, and it allows everyone to hear the wisdom of peers. But in most groups, total class discussion by itself is unsatisfactory because there is usually time for only a few to contribute.

Buzz Groups

Small groups of three to ten people are assigned any topic for discussion. They quickly select a chairperson and a secretary. The chairperson is responsible for keeping the discussion on track, and the secretary records the group's ideas, reporting the relevant ones to the total class.

Brainstorming

Students, usually in small groups, are presented with a problem and asked to come up with as many different solutions as possible. Participants should withhold judgment until all suggestions (no matter how creative!) have been offered. After a short break, the group should pick the best contribution from those suggested and refine it. Each brainstorming group will present its solution in a total class discussion.

Forum Discussion

Forum discussion is especially valuable when the subject is difficult and the students would not be able to participate in a meaningful discussion without quite a bit of background. People with special training or experience have insights which would not ordinarily be available to the students. Each forum member should prepare a three- to five-minute speech and be given uninterrupted time in which to present it. Then students should be encouraged to interact with the speakers, either directly or through a forum moderator.

Debate

As students prepare before class for their parts in a
debate, they should remember that it is the affirmative
side's repsonsibility to prove that the resolve is correct.
The negative has to prove that it isn't. Of course, the
negative may also want to present an alternative
proposal.

There are many ways to structure a debate, but the
following pattern is quite effective.

1. First affirmative speech
2. First negative speech
3. Second affirmative speech
4. Second negative speech
(brief break while each side plans its rebuttal)
5. First negative rebuttal
6. First affirmative rebuttal
7. Second negative rebuttal
8. Second affirmative rebuttal.

Floating Panel

Sometimes you have a topic to which almost everyone in
the room would have something to contribute, for
example: marriage, love, work, getting along with
people. For a change of pace, have a floating panel: four
or five people, whose names are chosen at random, will
become "experts" for several minutes. These people sit
in chairs in the front of the room while you and other
class members ask them questions. The questions should
be experience related. When the panel has been in front
for several minutes, enough time for each person to
make several comments, draw other names and replace
the original members.

Interview As Homework

Ask students to interview someone during the week and
present what they learned in the form of short reports
the following Sunday.

Interview in Class

Occasionally it is profitable to schedule an in-class
interview, perhaps with a visiting missionary or with

someone who has unique insights to share with the group. One person can take charge of the entire interview, structuring and asking questions. But whenever possible the entire class should take part. Each student should write a question to ask the guest.

In-Group Interview

Divide the class into groups of three, called triads. Supply all groups with the same question or discussion topic. A in the group interviews B while C listens. Then B interviews C while A listens. Finally C interviews A while B listens. Each interview should take from one to three minutes. When the triads return to the class, each person reports on what was heard rather than said.

Following every class period in which you use discussion, ask yourself these questions to help determine the success of your discussion time:

1. In what ways did this discussion contribute to the group's understanding of today's lesson?

2. If each person was not involved, what can I do next week to correct the situation?

3. In what ways did content play a role in the discussion? (I.e., people were not simply sharing off-the-top-of-their-head opinions.)

4. What follow-up, if any, should be made on the discussion? (For example, if participants showed a lack of knowledge, or misunderstanding in some area of Scripture, you may want to cover this subject soon during the class hour. Or, if they discussed decisions they were making or projects they felt the class should be involved in, follow-up outside the class hour may be necessary.)

STEP 4: *Focus on Life Response*

This step tries to incorporate a bridge from the Bible lesson to actual daily living. It should be a *specific* suggestion as to "how we are going to *do* something about this," either individually, or as a group. Though this is a goal to aim for, it is unlikely that everyone will respond to every lesson. But it is good to have a suggested life response ready for that one or two in the group who may have been moved by *this* lesson to respond *this week* in a tangible way.

Sometimes a whole group will be moved by one particular lesson to do a major project in light of their deepened understanding of, and commitment to, God's will. Such a response would be well worth the weeks of study that may have preceded it.

Examples of life response activities:

1. A whole class, after studying Scriptural principles of evangelism, decides to host an outreach Bible study in a new neighborhood.

2. As a result of studying one of Paul's prayers for the Ephesians, a group member volunteers to start and oversee a church prayer chain for responding to those in need.

3. A group member invites others to join her in memorizing the key verse for the week.

4. Two group members, after studying portions of the Sermon on the Mount, write and perform a song about peacemaking.

Obviously, only you and your group can decide how to respond appropriately to the challenge of living for Christ daily. But the possibilities are endless.

[1]From *Using the Bible in Groups*, by Roberta Hestenes.
© Roberta Hestenes 1983. Adapted and used by permission of Westminster Press, Philadelphia, PA.
[2]The material on discussion methods is adapted from *Creative Teaching Methods*, by Marlene D. LeFever, available from your local Christian bookstore or from David C. Cook Publishing Co., 850 N. Grove Ave., Elgin, IL 60120. Order number: 25254. $14.95. This book contains step-by-step directions for dozens of methods appropriate for use in adult classes.